Magical YA from UK Times Best-selling Author

JILL MARSHALL

BREATHE

A NOVEL

Jill Marshall Books

First published 2022
Copyright © Jill Marshall

A CIP catalogue record for this book is available from the National Library of New Zealand

ISBN 978-1-99-002498-6 Paperback

Jill Marshall Books

BREATHE

<u>A novel</u>

By

Jill Marshall

Chapter 1 Work Experience Day

Breathe, Sasha. Breathe, you idiot!

This is precisely what I tell myself as I pound along the pavement, late again, always late again, trying not to notice that my back jiggles with every step. Not my stomach (which doesn't just jiggle, it's sort of alive when I run, like a dog's bed squirming with puppies) or my thighs, which ripple from front to back as my trainers connect with the ground. Not even my butt, which rustles like a pair of sleeping bags at camp as one round buttock swishes, then the other. One then the other. One, swish; the other, swish.

No, none of that, although that's all happening. I notice only that my back, beneath my bra strap, is jiggling. I probably have back cleavage. I probably also have sweatiness galore, pouring down my back cleavage like rain along guttering and down the drainpipe, tipping perspiration onto my swishy buttocks. Drip, swish. Drip, swish. My body sounds like windscreen wipers.

Anyway, at least thinking about my jiggly back and buttocks like twin toddlers in sleeping bags and my drippy, sweaty perspiration – at least it all stops me thinking about what I'm late for.

Work Experience Day.

Now, don't get me wrong. There is nothing I'd like more than to miss Work Experience Day altogether. Nothing I'd like more than to imagine the whole day slipping by and nobody noticing that I haven't shown, and therefore nobody giving me a Work Experience for the week. Man alive, I actually WISH that could happen.

Unfortunately, though, there are dreams, and then there's life.

Even worse, there are dreams, then there are nightmares, and then there's my life.

What I'm doing by being late today (which is really not my fault, but I can't go saying that because nobody will believe me, and if they do they won't even care) is being late for *choices*.

It's first-come-first-served at Work Experience Day.

So what happens is this. Mrs Stewart reads out the list of potential places to work in order of brilliance and interest, and you stick your hand up and haggle for the best one – unless you happen to have grabbed yourself a job at Daddy's law firm, or Mummy's management consultancy. Which of course, I haven't. I'm sure they'd give me a job in their law firm or their management consultancy but they don't actually have those, owing to Mum being stuck at home and Dad being dead.

Ah well. C'est la vie. C'est ma vie. C'est le nightmare that is my vie.

I dream up what reasons I can give for being late and slow down to do it, making myself even more late. Really I slow down to let my lungs recover for a second - otherwise I will remove the need to explain my lateness by actually dying in the hallway. In the meantime, though, I do come up with a few thoughts:

Reason 1 – I missed the bus.

Reason 2 – I had to run and my back jiggled.

Reason 3 – I slowed down to avoid death-by-not-breathing.

Reason 4 – There's stuff that came before Reason 1 which I can't tell anyone about.

So I'll have to start with Reason 1 (they're all true, btw) and then get lambasted by Mrs Stewart for being tardy and irresponsible. Her words, not mine. If only she knew the small nightmare that is my vie. Totally not tardy. Terribly responsible.

Anyway, finally I'm at the school. I wave at the office lady who knows enough about me to not arrange her face into a stern scowl. Instead, she smiles sympathetically.

'They moved into the theatre,' she yells as I shuffle past, my trainers squeaking on the linoleum.

'Why?'

'Too many kids for the hall,' says Mrs Webb. 'Felix is already in there.'

Felix is her son, and sort of my friend, which is how she knows a fair bit about me.

'Okay. Thanks!'

I wave, running backwards so she won't be able to see my jiggle-back. She worries about me, I suspect, and witnessing jiggling of the back won't create a good impression at all.

At long last I reach the theatre. That's probably too grand a name for it. Don't go thinking it's got tiered banks of red velvet seats, or anything. It's really just a big square room with bleachers along three sides – any three sides, and sometimes not at the sides at all – and a collection of massive wooden boxes that can turn into a stage, or a runway, or sometimes, if stood up on their ends as they were for West Side Story the previous term, a pretend row of New Yoick tenement buildings.

Right now, two of the large wooden boxes are pushed together to form a platform. Mrs Stewart is perched on it, waving her pen around like a frumpy, middle-aged orchestral conductor. Her dress resembles a roll of floral wallpaper; her arms squeeze out through the holes at her shoulders like Play-Doh through one of those sausage machines, and as she points her pen at people, her bare white arms wobble. Suddenly I see myself in thirty-five years, and it is not a lovely sight.

'Sasha Baker, you're late,' she barks from the platform.

Everyone stops staring at the mesmerising bingo wings and turns to stare at me instead. I'm beetroot from running, and my shirt is sticking to me just about everywhere.

I smile. 'Sorry, Mrs Stewart. I missed the—'

'Best of the jobs,' she says with a sneer. 'You've missed all the work experience positions that might have suited you.' She pauses for a second, and I know she's working her way up to something good and nasty. 'All the sedentary office positions. All the supermarket check-out and shelf-filling opportunities. Most sadly of all, the customer service call centre positions, of which we had several, where the customers won't know who they're dealing with ...' Aha. Yep. Won't-know-they're-talking-to-a-blimp jobs. 'All. Gone.'

To be fair to the other students, nobody laughs outright. They know enough about bullying policies and zero tolerance not to pick on me for my jiggly bits, or anything else for that matter. Pity that Mrs Stewart doesn't seem to know about the policy, though. As long as she continues making horrible comments, it's like she's saying it's okay to have a go. Pick on the ones who don't get in there first.

Again, to be fair, she isn't only like this with me. *Anyone* who shows any sign of weakness, like, you know, being kind to lost Year Sevens or putting your hand up to ask for permission to go to the loo mid-lesson – they all get "lambasted" like me. Thank God I don't have a weak bladder on top of everything else. I'd be done for.

I stand there at the back of the theatre (or the side, or the front, or whatever it is) and avoid making eye contact with anyone, as Mrs Stewart carries on listing chubby-people jobs I could have done and haven't got, until even the populars – Chloe and India and that lot – are looking uncomfortable. I wonder what Work Experience they've scored. Chloe's job is probably in Daddy's law firm, as he actually has one. India – not sure, but she's very pretty, so maybe she's a model for the week. A professional WAG. Or Chloe Sevigny's personal assistant, or something, flown over to LA and given an expense account to buy clothes. More clothes.

Then I spot Felix. He's rolling his eyes at me, not in a 'Jeez, this woman can go on' kind of a way, but in a 'Jeez, Sash, open your mouth and say something' kind of a way. He even jerks his head towards her. I widen my eyes back at him in what I hope is a 'leave me alone, I'm okay' kind of a way.

Mrs Stewart is now on a major roll. She's listing jobs for me as Pie Seller, Performing Elephant, Opera Singer Who Can't Sing (not that she'd know, as I didn't even try for West Side Story even though Felix said I should, and insisted that major curves were *in* during the fifties). I can see she's quite enjoying it, even though my fixed smile is fading and I can feel tears prickling behind my eyeballs.

Then someone speaks up.

'What actual jobs ARE left, Mrs Stewart?'

Phew. Attention off me, and now onto the guy who has dared to interrupt Mrs Stewart in full flow.

Her head snaps round towards him. 'I'm sorry – you are?'

Hell, yes. You ARE!

He's the type of guy you notice. Chloe and India are so busy noticing they're practically bug-eyed. Super tall, really skinny but not in a "someone give that lad a meal" fashion, with blond hair that hasn't seen scissors in a long while and weird yellowy-green eyes above a long, regal-looking nose. Not incredibly good-looking – even a little off-putting with his eagle's eyes - but not ugly either, if you get my drift. Nice, in fact. Very, very nice.

He grins at Mrs Stewart. 'New boy,' he says, like anyone needs telling.

'And do you have a name, New Boy?' Just to look even more snazzy than usual as she stares at him, Mrs Stewart stows her glasses across her forehead in her own unique way that must have given birth to the name of "four eyes" for anyone wearing specs.

'Cass,' he says, pointing to her list with such easy confidence that his name will be on there despite being a) new and b) gobby, that I'm suddenly a tiny bit envious of him. And quite a large bit in awe of him. 'Cass Ely. Just transferred.'

It's a good job he's seven foot tall or whatever, as Mrs Stewart quickly spots what his finger is signalling. She frowns for a second, and then nods. 'Ah, here you are.'

He smiles at her again, and suddenly I realise that I'm smiling again, too. Properly now, not nervously and with an air of just-let-me-get-through-this. His cheerfulness must be catching.

'So … jobs? Which jobs are left?'

He's prompting her in a cheeky way that would get anyone else an instant detention. Felix is even making 'cut' signs at him across the floor, slicing across his neck with his right hand and trying to catch his eye from waist-level. Well, not quite waist-level, as Felix isn't *that* short, but from pretty low down on Cass's radar.

But to everyone's astonishment, Mrs Stewart just looks down at her paperwork again. Then she grins.

Nastily.

'Well, Cass Ely, there are two jobs left. And two people without placements – you and Sasha Baker. So that's very lucky.'

Oh no. Back in the spotlight. The two beams of light are directed at Cass on one side of the theatre, and me on the other. It's West Side Story gone wrong. Any minute now, the lights will pan across the audience and Cass and I will follow beneath them, directly under the beam, gawking at each other as the music starts and we take our places on the stage, ready to just burst into song. 'Cass Elyyyyyy; I just met a guy called Cass Elyyyy, and suddenly that name … will never be the same … to meeeeee …'

Only, of course, this isn't a film. This is life. My life. My terrible life.

And the whole room is holding its breath. What placements are left for the flabby girl with sweat rings, and the wonder boy from out of town?

'There's an admin stroke sales position,' says Mrs Stewart.

Yes! Admin stroke sales! I can do that! At least, I'm not entirely sure what it entails but it sounds okay. Sounds like I can just do talking. Cass is looking across the room at me, and I can see he wants me to take it.

'It's at the Sky Diving Centre,' ends Mrs Stewart triumphantly.

Oh.

Then the sniggers really do occur. Aloud and everything. Sasha Baker, doing sales at the Sky Diving Centre? No way. There's no way I can do that. I can feel myself trembling, just at the thought of walking through the door of the centre …

'What's the other one?' Cass jumps in quickly, and I think, awww, he's really nice. He's asking for me so I can avoid the Sky Diving role. I bet he's kind to Year Sevens and everything.

The teacher can hardly stop herself laughing. 'Working at The Body Beautiful.'

The Body Beautiful is a beautician's salon on the high street.

I am clearly not cut out to work in a beautician's, especially one called The Body Beautiful. If it was called 'Quite a Pretty Face' I might have gotten away with it, but not this.

'The job is cleaning,' adds Mrs Stewart, and suddenly all the attention is back on me, some eyes slightly sympathetic but most just mocking or even hostile. It's getting close to break time – people need their sugar fixes and I'm stringing this out for them.

This placement is the lowest of the low, really. Not even doing the beauty therapies, but cleaning. I'll be peeling wax strips bristling with human leg hair off the floor, picking up flannels speckled with squeezed blackheads, and worse … way worse than leg hair and blackheads, when you think about it.

Of course.

I should have known I'd get the horror job when I was late – not that it's my fault.

For a moment, even though I hate the idea with a passion that hurts, I consider sticking my hand up for the other one. Cass is staring at me across the theatre, his golden-green eyes conveying a message I can't understand. It's only then that I realise I have actually seen him before. Somewhere. Something about those eyes. I can't remember where though. The hospital, maybe?

Anyway, just as I'm willing my hand to lift itself up in the air and my mouth to open and shout out that I'll do the Sky Diving job, even though it will kill me to go in there, Mr Nice Guy gets in ahead of me.

'I'll go to the Sky Divers, then,' he said. 'Yep. Put me down for that. Sasha Baker can do the other one.'

Mrs Stewart nods smartly, and then flicks all the paperwork back into place on her clipboard. 'Good. Thank you, Mr Ely.' She doesn't thank me, strangely enough. 'So we're all done. Back to class, everyone, and please be sure to turn up promptly for your first day tomorrow. Promptly. That means *on time*, Ms Baker.'

'Yes, Mrs Stewart.'

There's probably no chance I'll be on time, but then there's every chance that I'll die of either heat exhaustion or embarrassment by the morning, so I figure there's not much point in saying anything.

Not much point at all.

I slouch out of the theatre behind the others, noticing that Cass's bird-of-prey eyes flicker across to me one more time before he strolls nonchalantly out of the double doors. Chloe, India and the others are hot on his trail with their flat midriffs and their ponytails temporarily removed from hairbands so that their hair swishes. Left and right, like my butt, only shiny and nice and smelling of coconuts.

Felix slides in beside me, saying nothing. He's good at that.

'What did you get?' I ask him.

'Mum got me a job,' he says.

I think about that for a moment, and then burst out laughing. 'Oh, Felix, the school office? You poor thing.'

'Tell me about it.'

So maybe I haven't got the worst placement of all. Just the most embarrassing. Just the one where everyone can peer in through the windows of beauty and jeer and point at me, skivvying on the floor festooned with hairy wax strips.

C'est la vie, I guess. C'est my terrible vie.

Chapter 2
Reason No 4, two hours before

Breathe in, Mum. That's it; all the way down into your stomach … a-a-a-a-a-and out. And in again, all the way down … a-a-a-a-a-and out.'

Mum does as she's told, though she frowns at me to show how much she hates having to be instructed in how to absorb oxygen by her school-aged daughter. She's nothing if not independent, my mum, despite everything. The thing is, if I don't tell her, she makes excuses like having to make breakfast for her girls and be an actual mother and so on, and then she forgets the exercises. And they're really meant to help.

'Sashaaaaa!' Olivia's voice bounces down the stairs. 'I can't find my Monday knickers!'

Mum interrupts her important breathing exercises to holler back at Olivia, trying to take ownership of the parenting again. 'So wear your Tuesday ones.'

'It's okay, Mum,' I tell her, and she scowls again but pats my hand at the same time. I fold my arms sternly and glare at her. 'I'll be two minutes. Now you keep breathing, okay?'

'I don't plan on stopping any time soon,' says Mum.

'In, all the way down, and out.'

'I do know how to breathe.'

'Just in case. I know old people become forgetful.'

Mum flicks me with the tea towel. 'I'm thirty-eight!'

'Like I said.' I grin at her. 'Old.'

The wailing from upstairs is increasing in volume. 'Sashaaaaaa!' Mum and I wince in unison and then I grab the laundry basket from the utility room and head upstairs.

Olivia is the world's loudest eleven-year-old. When it comes to her time to do work experience, assuming I'll still be looking after her by then, I'm going to suggest she's employed by the Fire Brigade. As a siren.

She's now loudly listing all the days-of-the-week underwear she can find that is everything but Monday, right through the closed door and down the stairs. 'I've got Thursday … no, hang on, that's Tuesday. Friday. Sunday. NOW I've got Thursday. Where is Monday?'

I open the door with one hip, as I'm balancing the laundry basket on the other. 'Are your Monday knickers white?'

Olivia gazes up at me from the chest of drawers which she has overturned onto the floor in the desperate search for Monday. 'How would I know?' she bleats. Loudly.

'You're obsessed with tiny details,' I remind her. 'Surely you'd remember something that obvious. Think about it.'

Frowning, Olivia holds up Friday (pink), followed by Thursday (yellow), Tuesday (green) and Sunday (black). Her face suddenly clears.

'Yes!' she bellows. 'Monday's knickers are white.'

'Okay, then,' I say, plonking the basket on her bed. 'The mystery of the Missing Mondays is solved, because Monday's undies are white, and therefore they are in this lot that I did yesterday, rather than the coloured undies which I washed on Saturday.'

I fish the elusive yet clean knickers out of the basket and place them on her head. 'Panic over?'

'Yes.' Olivia sighs, and even that is like a tornado ripping through the room. She pulls a pig-tail through each leg hole and remains cross-legged on the floor with the pants on her head, like a weirdly-dressed pixie. 'Thanks, Sash. And sorry.'

She smiles her goofy mad smile, and I can't be mad any more. Not that I was in the first place.

'I panicked. It's PE today, and I can't get changed in front of Danni and Tess with the wrong day's knickers on.'

I understand, of course. From what Livvy's told me, I can already guess that Danni and Tess are actually Chloe and India, five years younger. They'll have their underwear perfectly matched to the day, season and weather and the latest trend on after-school TV, and won't let Olivia forget about it if she gets it wrong. Particularly as she's still at the too-young-to-know-better stage of trying to be their friend.

I stack a small pile of white clothing on her bed and smile back at her. 'S'okay. Though I'd take them off your head if you really want to impress them.'

'No, really?' says Olivia, already speaking like Tess and Danni (I'm guessing) after only two terms, with way too much sass.

'Yes, really.'

I'm still standing there looking at her when I hear a key in the door, which is when I realise that I'm horribly late and it's Work Experience Day, and even if it makes matters better for Olivia, wearing the right knickers is not going to save me. Nothing will save me.

'Oh no, is George here already?' I grab the basket. 'Get dressed, Liv. You need to be out of the door in ten minutes at the latest.'

And I needed to be gone ten minutes ago. George is Mum's official carer, a big strapping woman called Georgina who's strong enough to lift Mum in and out of the wheel-chair and on and off the loo and onto the bed even without the hoists and get her to her MS support group and so on. She usually arrives after I've sorted Liv out and left for school myself, so now I'm guessing that I'm hideously, catastrophically late.

'All right, doll?' calls George as I scramble down the stairs.

'Late! Late again!'

'Thought so,' she says cheerfully, stashing her bag under the coat rack and peeling off her scarf and jacket. 'I'd give you a lift but I'm waiting for my insurance to clear.'

'Doesn't matter,' I say.

I sprint through the kitchen diner, wheeling Mum out of the way to her surprise and practically throwing the washing basket into the utility room, like a discus thrower at the Olympics. For the umpteenth time, I wish that I was at the same school as Olivia, just because it's closer and she can walk there. I'm not clever like Liv, though, so we didn't get the scholarship for it.

Anyway, enough with the self-pity. I kiss Mum on the cheek as I hurtle back through the kitchen, grabbing lunch and my backpack and a bit of bus money from the saucer of change on the table and shouting out instructions to George as I flap around putting my tie on.

'I made lasagne and froze it. It's on top of the mixed veg if Mum fancies that for lunch. She's done half her breathing and her specialist appointment is 1.30pm.'

Mum is waving the tea towel again, like a surrender flag. 'I can speak for myself, you know, Sasha.'

'I know, I know. Sorry.'

Sometimes with the MS, it's like I'm the mother and she and Olivia are the daughters, but she hates feeling like that, so I let her repeat word for word what I've just said to George as I try to find my Social Sciences homework. Eventually I retrieve it from beneath Olivia's laptop (another advantage of getting a scholarship) and shove it in my bag among the squashed egg sandwiches (ie sarnies that are squashed, not sarnies made of squashed eggs).

Then I call 'Bye' and 'Love you' and 'Thanks, George' to anyone who might be listening, and run out of the door. Run to the bus stop to find I've missed the number 28. Run to school to find I'm late for Work Experience Day, and I have back-jiggle. Run to the theatre to find there are only two jobs left, and new boy Cass Ely with the glorious eyes of golden-green takes the Sky Diving one so I'm stuck with cleaning at The Body Beautiful.

Still, at least I know plenty about cleaning. I've probably done more floor cleaning and washing of sheets and mopping up of bodily fluids than anyone in the whole school, including Mrs Stewart, so maybe it's a good thing I was late. The job will be a breeze, compared with Life.

Felix hangs about for me after Social Science to walk with me to the bus stop. Not that he gets the bus, or anything – he gets a lift home with his mum, but he has to wait for her to finish work before he's able to escape so sometimes he comes with me to distract himself.

'Aren't you going to wait in the office?' I say as he levers his shoulders off the wall until he's in an upright position. 'You could familiarise yourself with your new job.'

He lowers his eyelids disparagingly. Felix has these big, dark Italian eyes from his mum's side of the family. He can get more expression into the droop of an eyebrow or the shuddering close of the lids than Ryan Reynolds, and that is saying something as he is King in our household. We all have the hots for him, right from Olivia through to George, and that's a bit gross but what does he expect, being gorgeous and brilliant?

I wait for Felix to say something, but he doesn't. The squint is all I'm getting.

Meanwhile, though, I get an idea.

'Hey, maybe I should do that.'

'Wait in the office?' Felix stares at me, only half-joking.

'No,' I say, slamming him into the wall with a thrust of my wobbly hip. It doesn't bother me that Felix will feel the wobbliness. He's known me forever and will only object to being "bullied" rather than "hip-slammed by a hippo." 'Maybe I should go to The Body Beautiful and introduce myself.'

'Yes, you could tell them, "Hi, I'm Sasha, and I bully small boys,' says Felix, making a great big show of dusting brick dust off his sleeve.

'You're not a small boy.'

'I'm not a tall boy,' he points out, not without reason as he's a fraction of an inch shorter than I am.

'But *small* boy means *young* boy, like … four years old or something.'

'True.' He says it mildly, without argument or accusation, which is how he is most of the time apart from when I'm not speaking up for myself, like in the theatre. Right now, I'm actually volunteering to speak up for myself, so he can hardly argue. 'Yes, you should go. Tell them why you'll be late.'

'How do you know I'll be late?'

'You're always late,' he says. Then he glances at me. 'But you're allowed to say why.'

He's the one person, besides family members and his parents and some key medical staff like George, who knows about Mum. And Olivia. And Dad. When I was at primary school, we lived in the same street and were besties, sort of. Then we had to move to a house with disabled access, but I spent a lot of time in the school office over the years, chatting with his mother, and Felix would often be there. Saying very little. Taking it all in.

I won't, of course, tell The Body Beautiful people (the Bodies Beautiful?) why I'm not likely to be there on time, but in general it sounds like a good policy to go and see them now. I can warn them, at least. Let them know I'll make up the hours at the end of the day or something.

So instead of turning right to reach the bus stop and head home, I turn left to walk up the High Street. 'Coming?'

Felix nods. 'Try stopping me. Do you think I could get a free eyebrow wax?'

I laugh. He has eyebrows like Joe Jonas – or Groucho Marx, as he prefers it. 'How do you know about eyebrow waxing?'

Again, he says nothing, and instead simply raises one of the offending eyebrows in a quizzical expression of 'Wouldn't you like to know?'

We're getting pretty close to the beautician's now, after scuffling past the stationer's and the TAB betting shop and the Mini-Mart. The Body Beautiful is a couple of shop-fronts away, looking slightly tidier than its neighbours with a fresh coat of green paint and pale, frosted windows, apart from the name of the place which is etched in translucent glass. A row of crystals is dotted along the windowsill. Through the letter O, I can see a bored-looking receptionist prepared in day-glo make-up and enough fake tan to turn her the same colour as the wooden counter top.

She's also extremely tiny, as in skinny, in her tight-fitting white uniform. I suddenly worry that they'll make me wear something similar, only to discover they don't have it in my size.

I must be hesitating because Felix suddenly catches me by the elbow.

'Do it now,' he says.

'I can't.'

Suddenly it all seems very daunting even to be cleaning in such a place. It's like the emphasis is completely on BODIES, and BEAUTIFUL, and not at all on CLEANER, and I won't fit in. I won't fit in the white uniform, and I won't fit in the tiny rooms for tiny people, and I won't fit in generally.

But Felix steers me in through the door. 'That's an order, soldier,' he says, and then turns his spotlight eyes up the street.

Chloe, India and a couple of the other Wannabe WAGs from school are jostling their way along the payment, giggling noisily and flicking their hair into each other's faces.

I'm not sure whether they've seen me, but I'm through that door at lightning speed.

Boredy Beautiful on Reception glances up, then down, then up again, before attempting a glossy-lipped smile.

'Hi. Do you have an appointment?' she says.

'No, sorry.'

Why am I sorry? I don't need an appointment.

'I mean, I … I'm Sasha.' I hold out a hand and then snatch it back when I remember my nails. I've chewed them all down so far it looks like I'm a vampire who's been trying to scratch her way out of the coffin.

Boredy, to give her some credit, is not horrified, but seems a little unsure what to do. 'Sash-aaaaa,' she says, staring down at her appointment screen.

'No, sorry, I'm not … I'm doing work experience here for the next week. I'm the …' There is no way to dress this up, really. 'I'm the Work Experience Cleaner.'

Finally the light dawns.

'Oh! SASH-a.' Boredy sticks out her own hand. 'I'm Charlotte. I'm the apprentice.'

She's really nice, I realise. I'm not sure why this surprises me.

'It's going to be awesome having someone here my own age,' says Charlotte. 'Gets totally boring talking to old people all day. Some of the customers are, like, *forty*. Even FIFTY! They've got wrinkles and age spots and all sorts.'

'Not a problem,' I say, meaning it. She should see what Mum's got.

She hops down off her high, white stool. 'Annette's with a client at the moment, but do you want to look around?'

Feeling more comfortable by the second, I shake my head. 'No, that's okay. I just wanted to say hi and let you know I might be a tiny bit late in the morning—'

Suddenly there's a knocking at the window and I turn to see four long-haired visions of gorgeousness peering between the vowels in the word Beautiful, and I change my mind pretty quickly.

'Yes, I'd love to have a look round,' I say, and dive through the open door to the left of the Reception desk.

I'm guessing she'll follow me, but then the door jangles and I hear Chloe's voice flood in, like poisonous syrup.

'Hiiiii, Felix,' she says. 'Was that Sash I just saw?'

'No,' says Felix. 'I'm just here to book an eyebrow wax.'

I hear Charlotte make a run for the appointment book. The girls are giggling even more annoyingly now, and I'm trying to think of a way to walk back out into Reception and save Felix from Eyebrow Removal or everlasting shame when there's a quartet of squeals from the doorway.

'Did you see that?' says someone – Suzette, I think – and the others squeal again, so I guess they did.

'He looked straight in the window. Right at me!' That's India; I can tell by how she's sure it's all about her.

Felix and Charlotte, trapped by the reception desk, ask the question together. 'Who?'

'That new boy,' says India. 'Cass Ely.'

The four of them spit out another flurry of squeals, then I hear their heels clatter on the tiled floor as they all dash outside in pursuit of their golden-eyed prey. Felix stays behind, curiously chatty with Charlotte in a way I've never heard him before, explaining that he doesn't really want an eyebrow wax but then listening intently as she starts explaining the benefits to him.

'Right, right,' he's saying. 'Is that how you do your eyebrows? They're great. Nice … um … rainbow shape.'

It's peaceful back here. And there's not much to clean. With only a short corridor to explore, there's just one door to the left and right and a toilet at the end, facing me. From behind the door on the left, the combined sounds of tinkly music and gentle snores waft out, carried on a breeze of something that smells divine and summery.

The door on the right is slightly ajar. I push it open to check how much disgusting stuff is littered around the place, but it's empty apart from a high, narrow bed in the middle of the room, covered in white sheets and a soft beige blanket, and a set of low shelves to one side with a few jars and bottles arranged along the top. The same tinkly music is being piped into the room, and I tune into it as I step across the room to check the sheets. Will I have to clean those, I wonder? Whoever has done it already has made a very nice job of these.

The music is lilting and lovely, and I realise how pleasant it is not to have to concentrate on any lyrics … although there does seem to be a voice whispering in the background. I listen harder.

Lie down, it seems to be saying.

Lie on the bed, Sasha.

Well, it has been a hard day. Harder than usual in my generally hard life. I'm yawning already.

Before I have time to stop myself, I accept the invitation and snuggle down onto that soft, furry blanket, and as the voice becomes clearer I feel as though I know it. I've heard that voice before, so I listen even more.

'Relax and breathe,' it seems to be saying. 'Relax … and breathe. And breathe. And sleep.'

I love that room. Absolutely love it.

And I know, even as I drift off into slumber, that I never, ever want to leave.

Breathe. That's it, head between knees. Deep breath, Sasha. Suck it in. Come on!'

I appear to be having some kind of out-of-body experience, because the voice telling me to breathe is not the same smooth, lullaby tones of the treatment room at Body Beautiful. Instead it's some man yelling at me in kind of an angry manner.

I lift my head to look straight into the bulbous eyeballs of a guy in his twenties. 'Don't stop!' he roars into my face, so I drop my head again and start breathing like it's going out of fashion.

Eventually I manage to whisper from where my chin is buried in my boobs: 'What's going on?'

'Just a panic attack,' snaps the guy. 'Happens all the time. It's scary stuff if you're not particularly … active,' he finishes, and I know he's being careful with his words.

I'm plenty active, I want to say. You try looking after your mum with a debilitating disease and your eleven-year-old sister who has no social boundaries, doing the

30

washing and the cleaning and quite a lot of cooking, and calling the emergency services when necessary. But I know exactly what he means. He's means "fit" in a normal way, like someone who plays tennis at the weekend and eats steak and greens the whole time because their parents can afford it.

I'm just trying to decide whether to speak up or not (Felix would be proud that I'm even considering it) when I realise that I don't actually owe this dude any explanations, because I genuinely have no idea who he is.

In fact, I've got no idea where I am.

'Ten more,' he raps sharply. 'In. Out. In and out. That's it. Out. In. Out.'

I sneak a glance at him between my knees as I huff like a dog on a hot day. He's wearing laced-up black boots, like Docs but aggressively shiny, with blue cotton trousers tucked into them. There's a black leather belt around his waist cinching in a matching blue cotton shirt. I wonder if his mother dresses him, until I work out it's a boiler suit of some kind. Over the top of the shirt lies a pair of braces. Braces? Who wears braces these days? It's a very weird outfit. Maybe I'm light-headed from over-breathing, and it's really just a teacher, or a Year 13 in uniform.

'And out. Right. Try standing up.'

This time I am allowed to lift my head. I blink blearily as my surroundings swim into view, and the guy who has been forcing me to eat my own chest offers me a hand to get off the floor. Right then, I stare at his braces, and it clicks what they are.

Not braces.

Straps.

Straps that actually make sense of the weird outfit, because the outfit really is a uniform like the one they wear in the Air Force, and the straps are part of it because they belong to the thing attached to his back.

His parachute.

No. Actually, OUR parachute.

This is a horror story come true. For some reason which I cannot begin to explain, I am back at Sky Divers on one of the official Worst Days of My Life, my terrible life, with this buffed-up nobody who is going to tandem sky-dive with me. With me, Sasha Baker, strapped to his chest like a hideous overgrown baby in one of those pouches.

'What am I doing here?' I mutter, my eyes swivelling left and right.

What I mean, of course, is what am I doing back at Sky Divers with Angry Airforce Dude when I should be snoozing at the Body Beautiful, but I guess there's no way he can answer that.

Instead, he points into the space over my shoulder.

'Well, I thought,' he says in a low voice, 'that you'd prefer to have the heebie-jeebies over here on your own, instead of with all your classmates.'

Heart pounding, I chance a quick glance over my shoulder - and then my eyes close in shock.

Classmates. They're all there. Chloe and India and Suzette, of course, looking like Little Mix in their matching outfits, and Felix and his friend Sam on either side of them like gargoyles, short and bunched up and totally not created to pull off sky-diving gear. Another half-dozen students are swapping impatiently from one foot to the other, waiting for me to get going.

I know now, without a shadow of a doubt, exactly where I am. It's Activities Afternoon, where we all have to try something stretching and life-affirming like working with the homeless, or mountaineering.

Or in my case, falling out of a plane with a shouty man strapped to my back.

What's weird, though, is that this … this whole event all happened more than two months ago. I must be dreaming. I *hope* I'm dreaming. Wake up, Sash, I tell myself – inwardly, in case it isn't a dream. The guy's hand on my shoulder strap seems pretty darn real, and so does the low-pitched drone of the plane's engine as it idles on the tarmac outside the hangar.

Felix is doing eye-telepathy with me. *Come on, Sash. Pull it together. Please.*

It's for my sake, not his, that he wants me to pull it together.

I remember why, too. In a few moments, I'm going to cross the concrete towards the doors, take one look at the plane, and then cause a general hold-up because I'm too scared to get in the thing. Terrified. And it's not a normal terror like anyone might experience when launching themselves voluntarily out of a floating object 10,000 metres up in the air. No. It's my very own, very specific Sasha Terror.

Which I totally want to get under control.

Catching Felix's eye, I wink, hoping that he gleans from this that I'm okay, that I *have* got it under control, and I'm not going to ruin it for everyone.

And I try. I really do. Even when I haven't a clue why or how I'm freshly back in this not-so-fresh hell, I realise something. I'm getting a chance at a do-over. I can make it this time.

So after gulping in yet more fume-soaked air, I stand up straighter and attempt a smile at Angry Maverick. 'Sorry. I'm ready now.'

He stares, not believing a word of it, but then eventually he nods and we sidle back over to the group. Well, I sidle. He goose steps.

'Right, panic over,' he shouts at a volume that would even impress Olivia. 'Back to business. As I was saying before S… as I was saying, we're going to go up in small groups of four. Each of you will be safely buckled to your sky-diver, and they'll help you follow the drill we've all been through. Sasha,' he adds coldly, 'you'll be with me.'

The look of relief on the other sky-divers' faces is obvious, and they launch themselves at the Swishy Quartet at speed. Quite rudely, I think. I realise – no, I remember – that Ian (yes, that's his name, it's coming back to me now) is stuck with me because he's the leader and they get the clients with the most issues – panic attacks, vertigo, straining boiler suits that might split in mid-air …

I can do this. This time, I can do it. To be honest, I'd been really sorry last time (or was it this time?) that I'd not been able to go through with it, and now I could change the past. Present. Whatever.

'Steel yourself, Baker,' I hiss under my breath. 'Make it happen.'

'You can do this, Sasha Baker,' says a voice behind me.

For the tiniest moment I think it's the instructor actually being NICE, but then I turn around and it's not even him.

'What are you doing here?' I say, the surprise making me a teensy bit abrupt.

It's Cass Ely.

'Just thought I'd observe,' he says, watching me down his beakily beautiful nose with those amberlicious eyes.

'But you're new.' This isn't making sense. 'In two months' time, you're new.'

He laughs and scratches his head. 'I think you might need more oxygen.'

'But I—'

'Oh,' he says suddenly, dropping from his enormous height to the floor. 'Your lace is undone.'

And he ties it, right there in the hangar, like Prince Charming altering Cinderella's slipper to fit. The Swishers have spotted this, and India is doing her best to get her phone out of her bag. Whether it's to take a photo of this Beauty and the Beast combo, or dash over to Cass demanding his phone number, I'm not sure. Either way, though, it won't work out well for me.

Fortunately, Felix has been so busy staring at Cass that he doesn't spot her in time. He trips over her doubled-up body, sending them both sprawling. All attention snaps back to the mound of bodies and sky-diving equipment squirming around on the floor.

'There,' says the mysterious Cass Ely. 'You're done.'

Before I have chance to thank him, Ian is bellowing orders again. I'm sure he's deeply regretting taking on this particular group. We're nothing but trouble, what with Shallow-breathing Sasha and the Tumbledowners. With a small jolt of anguish, I notice that I seem to be the cause of much of the mayhem.

I so don't want to be the cause of any mayhem. Really, if I could never get noticed for anything and just be left to get on with my life in complete anonymous invisibility, I'd be far happier.

And talking of invisible, Cass has disappeared, so I waddle after Ian in my strange harness and catch his arm.

'I'm ready, Ian.'

Will not cause mayhem. Will not cause mayhem.

I want to convey this to him, somehow, but he just sighs and rounds up the rest of the class. 'Come on. Girls first. That's you, too, Sasha.'

I do realise I'm a girl, I want to say, but that would be a little mayhemmy, and anyway, he's already herding us towards the plane. Then I'm climbing the steps. Hurrah! This is already further than I got last time. Then we're inside the plane and taking our seats and buckling up and listening to the engine rev and then whizz and then whine as the plane bumps across the runway and starts its ascent.

I feel like yelling aloud: I'm doing it! I don't know how this weird chance has come about, but I'm pretty thrilled about it. When everyone stomps their feet and bellows, following Ian's orders to "Make some noise, gang!" I even join in.

That's when I notice it. There's something strange hanging off my shoelace. I can't get my foot close enough to study it properly, but it looks like some kind of token with symbols inscribed across it. Maybe Cass tied a good luck charm to my foot!

But then a shaft of sunlight glances off it and I notice that it's shaped like an envelope with a diamond across the centre. Kind of like a … a pentacle, or something. So maybe it's not a charm. Perhaps it's a curse.

That would explain a lot, to be honest.

And even as the plane is bouncing through the light cloud cover, I feel the terror take over me in a cold sweep that drenches me in sweat from head to my cursed foot.

What if I don't make it? I'm scared of dying.

I can't die.

Not because of death itself, or because jumping out of a moving aeroplane is a mad thing to do by anyone's standards, but because I'm the only one holding our family together. How will Olivia get herself organised if I absent-mindedly die on her, just because of Activities Afternoon? How will Mum cope in the evenings when George leaves or in the morning before she arrives? Who'll talk to Gran and visit Dad's grave and do the washing and everything else?

I can't afford to die.

And anyway, haven't we had enough death already?

So I grab Ian's arm, just the same way as I did the last time I was in this hideous situation and caused a fuss, only now I'm doing it at ten thousand feet. My eyes fill with tears, and with Felix-like optic telepathy I try to let Ian know that I can't jump. I just can't.

Oh, and also I'm gonna be sick. I don't need to tell him this as it's written all over my face, and then it spatters across his Gestapo outfit.

We end up back on the ground, with four mutinous Skydivers staff and Chloe, India and Suzette staring daggers at me because none of them could jump with me not being well. Especially when I was not well all over their feet.

Felix pats me on the shoulder as the groups pass each other. 'Next time,' he whispers.

But we both know there'll never be a next time. Not again. One second chance is surely all you ever get, and I've blown mine.

And Cass Ely is nowhere to be seen, which is pretty rich when I know deep down that somehow, it's all to do with him.

Chapter 4 Now-ish

Breathe it, believe it, be it and you'll see it,' Felix is saying to Charlotte as I skid back into the Reception area.

Great. I've woken up after a living nightmare in desperate need of some Felix calm sanity, and instead he's quoting lyrics from The Lampshades' latest to a skinny orange beauty queen.

Then I remember that she's nice, and I feel less aggravated. Though totally in need of Felix and his sensible eyebrows. Thank goodness they're still on his face, and not attached to a waxing strip in the bin behind the reception desk.

Charlotte smiles at me, her expression sweetly enquiring. 'Did you manage to have a look around? I'm sorry Annette's not available to give you a head start, but if I can tell you anything—'

'How long was I gone?' I blurt out.

Oops. I'm being mayhemmy again, just like I was back then. Two months ago.

Also, I sound a little rude, like I'm questioning just how much I could possibly have discovered at the back of The Body Beautiful in maybe two seconds flat.

Felix frowns, his eyebrows marching towards each other at a hearty pace. 'About ninety seconds,' he says, checking the clock behind Charlotte's head. 'Long enough for me to discover that waxing sounds painful and that I look a bit like Connor from that band that sings "Breathe it, believe it."'

'The Lampshades,' say Charlotte and I together. She glances at me and giggles, then yells, 'Jinx!' in a too-loud fashion that suggests I was meant to say it at the same time.

'I'm always so slow at that,' I tell her with a grimace. 'My sister's constantly beating me to it.'

Charlotte nods knowingly, her earrings glinting in the bright neon light. 'I've got twin sisters, aged thirteen. They're practically the same person. I don't get a look in!'

'Ouch,' I say, and Charlotte laughs. She is just really, really nice. Why am I at school with the Swishy Quartet instead of *nice* beautiful people?

Anyway, this is just one of the many million questions I now have zipping around in my brain, but at the top of the pile is the one about what happened when I dropped off on the high bed in Treatment Room 2. I must have dropped off, surely, or had a little brain attack or something. This is not to be taken lightly – Mum has little brain attacks and moments when she can't remember what was going on or is so tired she falls asleep mid-sentence, and suddenly I'm scared that Mum's MS is hereditary, and I've started to become ill. I can't be ill, for all the same reasons I can't carelessly fling myself out of a plane and potentially die. Obviously I can't ask Mum about it because I'll upset her, but I have to find out somehow.

Luckily, even if I can't ask my mum, I can ask someone else's.

'Let's head back to school,' I suggest to Felix after waving goodbye to Charlotte and promising to be there as soon as I can in the morning.

'Seriously?' Felix shakes his head mournfully. 'You want me to spend *more* time with my mother?' He checks himself quickly, conscious as ever that we never really know how long I'll get to spend with mine. 'Sorry.'

'Not your fault,' I say. 'Not anybody's fault. But I've just had this very weird experience at the back of the salon, and I want to check that it's not … you know, a sign.'

'A sign of what?'

'A sign of genetic diseases.'

Now his eyebrows form a pyramid shape in the middle of his forehead. He really could a whole presentation in eyebrow mime. 'Really? What can have happened in the time you were out of Reception? It was only about a minute.'

I'm about to tell him what happened as we swing past the stationer's again, en route back to school, when I spot the person who made my dream especially weird. Cass

41

Ely is leaning against a lamp-post, one foot flat along it so that the knee in one impossibly long leg is bent. With that beaky nose, he looks like a flamingo. Not that the Swishers seem to care; they're all flicking their hair around him at such speed that it's a wonder they aren't taking off.

Okay, so he's a hot flamingo.

He appears to be a little bored by whatever India is showing him on her phone, and catches my eye across the top of her head. With a shrug, he answers my unspoken question, which is basically, 'What's a hot flamingo to do when four gorgeous girls are practically dribbling on him?'

Or at least, he obviously thinks that's what my unspoken question is. But it's not. Feeling unusually unafraid of talking to the new guy, I startle Felix by taking off across the road in Cass's direction. A taxi blasts its horn at me, and the heads of the Chloe Crew turn as one as the driver leans out to shout abuse. Felix follows me and holds up a finger to silence the driver – not aggressively, just as in 'Don't you dare.' I know the driver is swallowing the words "fat" and "cow" and "stupid" but somehow I don't care as I hurry the last few paces through the traffic.

'Cass Ely,' I say, unable to think of anything wittier.

The green-gold eyes narrow. 'Sasha Baker,' he says back, with no hint of irony at all. He's remembered my name, all the way from this morning. That's amazing.

Clearly India, Suzette, Chloe and Dana think so too, as they all glare at me and then fluff their hair out some more to block me from his view. 'Gosh, we haven't even introduced ourselves properly,' Chloe is gushing, piqued that someone might not know her name in full. 'I'm Chloe Shawford, and this is In—'

'Excuse me, Chloe Shawford,' says the new guy, 'but I think Sasha Baker wants to talk to me.'

'You don't, do you, Sasha?'

Suzette is the only one who seems to have recovered from the blatant interruption of their leader with the full power of speech. Now she's looking at me with that cock-hipped, arms-folded, head-tilted dare of an expression written all over her. I'm not sure if she's asking me if I don't want to talk to him or telling me. Scratch that. I'm sure she's telling me.

And now that the question is out there, I'm wondering if I do actually want to talk to him. What am I going to say? Cass Ely, why did you pop up in my dream a few minutes ago? Yeah. Like that's never been said to him before.

But they're all staring at me now, even Felix who has finally placated the taxi driver and the rest of the traffic and is standing at my side, eyes flicking between me and Cass Ely and the goal defence line-up of Chloe, Dana, India and Suzette.

Cass Ely pushes himself away from the lamp-post and breaks through the chorus line of girls. 'You do want to talk to me, I can see that.' He smiles encouragingly. 'Shoot.'

'Well, I …' Okay, Sasha, you set yourself up for this one. What am I supposed to say now? 'I wanted to … um … thank you for … this morning.'

'Pleasure,' he states briefly. 'And what else?'

'I … um …' There's this question floating around at the back of my mind, but I can't quite seem to catch hold of it. 'It's just …' Yes, it's there. Did I know him from the hospital or somewhere? Or had he been at the school during the sky-diving trip? 'You seem familiar. Do I … have we met before? Before this morning, I mean?'

Chloe stuffs her hair in her mouth to stop herself from laughing, but India is less subtle.

'Seriously, Sasha – haven't we met before somewhere? Is that your best line?'

The girls all hoot with hysterics.

I shake my head quickly. 'I don't know what you mean. It's not a … a line.'

It's dawning on me fast, of course. They think I'm trying to chat him up. As if I, Sasha Baker with the back-jiggle and the complicated home life, would ever dream of marching up to the new boy, the golden new boy, to ask him out. I wouldn't ask anyone out. Why would I even dream…

Cass, to his credit, just ignores them. 'Yes,' he tells me in his matter-of-fact way. 'You've seen me before.'

'I don't think she has,' says Felix, as if he knows every single thing about me.

'At the … school?' I don't dare ask him if it was at the sky-diving centre. That would be too weird.

'At various places, at various times,' says Cass enigmatically. The girls all gasp, and Cass shrugs. 'It's a small town,' he explains.

'But we've never seen you before,' whines Dana, trying desperately to get his attention away from me and back to the four stellar girl-specimens who deserve to be swept up in his beaky golden gaze. 'Have we?'

And Cass Ely shrugs again.

'You're not Sasha Baker,' he tells Dana, which is obviously true, but is so bewildering a statement to all who are hearing it that the six of us who aren't seven-feet tall all look at each other, trying to work it out.

Darkness is beginning to gather, and as the chill sets in as the light disappears, I can suddenly sense that, without even trying, I've become their enemy. These four powerful girls, who have had very little need to even bother with me before today, now have cause to hold me in their attention. Cass Ely has noticed me, for some reason which I can't explain, and that is not to be forgiven.

Cass watches our silent exchanges from his great height, then says, 'Nice to see you all, guys. I've got to go.'

'Where?' cries India, a little too shrill. She repeats herself with a hand on his arm. 'Where are you off to? We're going to Dana's for a game of pool; want to come with?'

'No, thank you.' Cass smiles briefly at Dana rather than India, and then nods to me. 'Good luck tomorrow, Sasha,' he says.

Stop talking to me stop talking to me stop talking to me, I think. But of course, I'm too polite to tell him that he's about to be the cause of even more social isolation than I already suffer, so I nod at him. 'You too. All of you,' I add quickly.

But it's too late. The dice has been rolled. As the new target of everyone's affection lopes off into the sunset, it's my turn to run.

'Come on, Sash, Mum's going to be expecting us.'

Felix grips my elbow and I jump out of my skin for the millionth time that day. What is happening to me and my nervous system?

'Yep,' says Chloe, although it doesn't sound as if she's agreeing with Felix. 'Mummy's waiting. Run along, Sasha.' She pushes her pore-free nose close to mine.

Felix steps between us, sensing the atmosphere. 'That's not what I meant, Shawford.'

'It's all right, Felix,' I mutter under my breath. 'I'd better get home anyway.'

Only Felix knows why, of course, and I want to keep it that way. Because if those girls discover what my life is like at home, it will be another chink in my armour. And now they have me on their radar, I'm going to have to keep that armour as polished and chink-free as possible.

'I'll walk you,' says Felix flatly, and somehow, despite him being shorter than me and with comedy eyebrows,

46

I'm very glad of his company to the garden gate and the sloping ramp that leads to the door.

They're not following us or anything, but I can't help feeling that someone, somewhere, is watching.

'Come to school early if you want to use the computer,' says Felix.

'Computer?'

He frowns. 'Infection diseases,' he says, reminding me of what I'd been going to do before the sighting of Cass Ely stole my brain.

'There's probably no chance of being early,' I tell him.

'Okay. Just try, or we can do it after work, if you want,' he says. 'I'll be in charge of the office, don't forget.'

I raise a hand, hardly able to take in the events of this strange day. 'Thanks, Felix.'

He does a Mexican wave with his eyebrows and disappears into the dusk.

Chapter 5 That evening

'Breathe meaningfully and joyfully. Breathing is a key part of meditation,' I read aloud from Olivia's homework. 'Why are you meditating at school?'

Olivia rolls her eyes. 'We're doing mindfulness?' It's not a question, but everything she says when she comes back from school goes up at the end, just to let me and Mum know that we're idiots. 'It's all part of being a rounded person?'

I can see that Mum would like to have a go at her but is feeling too tired tonight. I'm a bit tired myself after the freak-show that has been my day, and the nightmare that is my life, but c'est la vie. And anyway, I'm already a rounded person. That's half the trouble.

'Okay,' I say gently, 'well, I can't help you with mindfulness, but I can do some French with you.'

Olivia's eyes are on the roll again. 'We're starting with Latin?' I guess that's what happens when you get scholarships and go to posh schools.

I shrug, feeling more than a little helpless. 'I've never done Latin.'

'Never mind,' drones Olivia. 'It's not much anyway. I'll do it myself after tea. What are we having?'

Tea. Food. I haven't thought about that yet. It's actually a good job I'm off to work experience tomorrow, as there wouldn't have been time to do normal homework and stuff for myself as well as being chief cook and second mum.

Mum smiles at me sadly, so evidently regretting that she can't do more to help that I hate myself for a moment. I pull myself together. 'Mum, did you have that lasagne at lunchtime?'

'No. George made us a ham and cheese toastie.'

That'll be all the cheese gone then. I write down "CHEDDAR" on the wipe-off list near the fridge, and ferret around in the freezer for the lasagne I made at the weekend. 'Okay to have it tonight then? There should be enough for your lunch tomorrow if you have it with salad.'

Mum smiles again, a bit more energetically. 'Great!'

'Awww, I had carbs for lunch,' moans Olivia.

'You had what?'

'A big pile of carbs? Baked potato with tuna and mayo?'

This is not Olivia talking. This is the Right-Knickers Girls. Normally Olivia couldn't tell if you'd passed her the cereal box and she'd been chewing the cardboard. But now that she's at her new school, mindfulness and fewer carbs will be all the rage. I'll have to change the shopping list completely if she carries on.

'I'll give you more salad,' I tell her.

'That's just carbs too,' she says with another eye roll, but it's a mini one this time and I can see she's easing off on her campaign to be difficult.

'But at least they're green.'

'It's not the colour that makes a difference?'

'Oh good. I'll give you beetroot then.'

She hates beetroot. 'Don't you dare!'

I bat at her with her meditation guide. 'I don't even buy beetroot, you moron.'

Back to her usual sweet self, Olivia sticks her tongue out at me and slobs out of the room. 'Yes, I'll set the table,' she groans to Mum who doesn't even have to say anything, just raises her eyebrows at my sister as she pushes past the wheelchair. 'Half an hour, sis?'

'Make it forty-five minutes. It's a big lasagne.'

'You're a big lasagne,' she snaps. She darts out of the way before the cushion I've fired off can hit her.

And suddenly it's just me and Mum in the room, viewing the trail of litter and discarded school gear that Olivia has left in her wake. It's as if an entire ticker-tape parade has just marched through the room.

'How does she do it?' I ask, shaking my head as I begin picking up the stuff I will just need to pick up again by the morning.

Mum laughs. 'How do *you* do it?'

'What?'

'You know,' she says with a sad smile, and I know she means … everything. How do you do everything and stay cheerful and manage to even offer to do homework with your little sister. 'I did a bit of Latin at school,' she tells me suddenly. 'Maybe I can help Liv with it. I just need to remember some …'

She squints at the ceiling as if she's trying to project some Latin onto it from her brain, and I want so much to ask her what it's like – to have brain attacks and not recall things that you once knew very well. Mostly I want to ask her if it's genetic and could be passed on to me and maybe even Liv. Maybe loudness is a symptom! Instead of all that, I peel cling-film off the lasagne dish as I pre-warm the oven.

'How was Work Experience Day?' she asks. I'm surprised she's remembered that, not because of her brain blips but because I'd tried not to mention it. 'Did you tell them you already do work experience every single day?'

Ah. So that was why she'd remembered it.

I laugh as if it's funny when it isn't. 'Yes, and they said that's fine then, I don't have to do any more. I'm having the week off.'

Mum stares. 'Really?'

I turn my back on her as I shove the lasagne into the oven, so she can't see my face. 'Not really. I'm going to help out with cleaning and stuff at the Body Beautiful on the High Street. I went down there to introduce myself and this girl called Charlotte was there and she's really sweet.

51

The owner's called Annette and I haven't met her yet but it all looks really good and I'm totally okay with it.'

I'm talking too much, and she knows it.

'I'm sure they can find you something else, Sash.' Her voice has the helpless tone to it that comes out when she wants to be 'Proper Mum' but can't. 'I could call the school?'

'No way,' I tell her, mock sternly. 'Felix is threatening to have his eyebrows waxed there. I am not missing that for anything.'

'Oh well. I wouldn't either.' She's half-relieved, half-sad that she won't get to speak to the school on my behalf. 'In fact, if you're selling tickets, I'll take one. Two – one for Olivia as well.'

I act as if I'm considering it. 'I'll let you know. And don't worry about me going there, Mum. It's …' Freaky. Weird. Filled with mind-control substances that are piped into the treatment rooms along with the tinkly music. 'Interesting. And Charlotte's nice. I think I'm going to enjoy it.'

Which is the weirdest thing of all, because that's actually true. No school. Nice Charlotte. Tables to sleep on during the day. What's not to like?

Unfortunately, my words have had the wrong effect on Mum. She's suddenly crying, reaching for my hand to pull me onto the chair beside her. I sit down, bewildered. 'What? Shouldn't I go there?'

'No!' She waves her hand in front of her face – her good hand, that still responds to brain orders. 'I'm being silly. It's just that you haven't had much to enjoy for these last couple of years, have you?'

She's going to talk about it, I know. The thing I don't want to talk about.

'Not since … since …'

Since Dad died, she's going to say. Since Dad came home bone-white with anxiety, crouching low beside Mum's chair and burying his head in her shoulder and horror of horrors starting to cry, telling her that he'd lost his job, lost it two weeks before because of all the time he was taking off with her MS getting worse, but he'd been going out every morning as usual because he didn't know how to tell her and because he was walking and walking the streets, looking for jobs, any job, anything to keep his family together.

That Night, when everything changed …

And I don't want her to talk about it, because it makes her so sad and because it's not even true that I haven't enjoyed anything since then.

So I interrupt her.

'Puberty,' I say with a nod.

'What?'

'I haven't had any fun since puberty. You should have warned me, Mum. Periods are a bitch.'

'Sasha!' She lets out a shocked little bark of laughter. 'Since when have you said things like that?'

'Since—'

'Puberty,' we say together.

I rub her hand. 'And by the way, just imagine how much worse that's all going to be with Olivia.'

We gaze at each other, picturing the lolling and groaning and yelling and general dramatics that will go on when Olivia's periods start. Then Mum shakes her head. 'Okay. I'm moving out before that.'

'Me first.'

'You've got nowhere to go. I can escape to the hospital.'

'True. You're so lucky,' I tell her.

And we both laugh again, because she's not lucky at all, and neither am I, but somehow we make it all work.

This evening, it all works too. Just as usual. I dish up tea, Olivia sets the table at the very last moment so the last fork goes down exactly as the food arrives, Mum wheels herself across to the head of the table and tries to make us say grace like she has every evening since That Night, and Liv and I make jokes about it but gently refuse … and then we eat and chat; do some homework, watch a bit of TV and shout at the screen, before George pops back in to help Mum into bed because she can't manage that by herself (although she can usually get herself up in the morning and uses her cane until breakfast unless she's extra tired), and I clear up the Olivia bomb-trail yet again yet again yet again before swabbing down the kitchen as if it's an operating theatre so Mum doesn't pick up any extra germs.

As I'm putting the lasagne tray in the dishwasher (pre-soaked and with all the knobbly burnt bits scraped off to make it worth dishwashering), I look around the kitchen and say a little grace of my own. Thank you for Mum and Liv. Thank you for this house that works for us. Thanks really heaps for George. Thanks for letting me do my work experience with Nice People. Thanks for friends like Felix. Thanks for new guys who stand up for me – or do they? Maybe they get me into trouble … but anyway, thanks …

Just as I think these thanks, not even quite sure who I'm thanking, I glance at the window. My heart nearly stops. Just for a second I see someone. I think it's him, I think it's Dad, sneaky-peeking in on his way to the back door like he always did, to catch a beautiful family moment …

Of course, it's not Dad. But it is someone.

I can't swear to it, but it's as if someone tall with really blond hair whisked out of sight before I could spot him properly. My chest thumps and I consider all the alarms around the house for Mum to alert the hospital – can I just call the police?

And what exactly would I say?

'Hey, police officer, I think the new guy at school, Cass Ely, is a crazy stalker.' 'And why do think that?' 'Because he knows my name, and I think he might have been in my back garden a moment ago. But also he may not be as new a guy as I thought because I seem to have met him two months ago.'

Yep. That would go down well. I'd just sound weird.

So instead of calling for help, for some wild reason and without even thinking about it, I grab the lasagne dish and race for the back door, adrenalin pumping behind my ears as I yank it open, pound onto the doorstep, brandish the oven-proof dish at tall beaky almost-strangers with a blood-curdling yowl …

There's nobody in the floodlit yard. Which is just as well, as I don't know how much damage a medium-sized piece of bake-wear could actually do.

But as I inspect the floor for footprints, I notice something that makes me feel even more uneasy.

The token thingummy that Cass Ely attached to my shoe in the Body Beautiful dream glints in the moonlight. It's here, in this world, in the now. Tied to my actual shoe, on my very own foot.

I can't explain how that's happened. I was dreaming, wasn't I?

But the little envelope with a diamond in the middle winks up at me, and I know that if I touch it, it will be hard and present and very, very real.

So I step on the heel of my shoe with the other foot and pull it off without untying the laces, and leave it outside the door as if I've stepped in dog dirt. Then just to be sure one shoe hasn't infected the other half of the pair, I do the same with the other one even though it is token-less, before locking the door very carefully and taking the lasagne dish to bed with me.

I take Olivia's mindfulness book too. Might as well figure out how to be a more 'rounded' person. After all, there'll be no sleeping tonight. Not after all that. I lie in the dark with my eyes open, listening to the beating heart of the house as it settles slowly into the night. Thuddum. Thuddum. Thuddum. No sleeping. No sleeping for me. No sleeping …

Chapter 6_Night-time

Breathe in right to the bottom of your ribs. That's right. Down to your diaphragm. Let your belly stick out.' A man laughs. 'Don't be self-conscious, it's very natural.'

I lift one eyelid warily. I'm still asleep, right?

Wrong. I'm staring at the chipped flooring of the school gym. Hell. Is it Ian the goose-stepping parachutist again? I squint right. No. More feet. More dangling heads. A whole row of them.

'Okay,' says the man again. I recognise his voice this time. It's Mr Battersby, the music teacher. Why's he doing Phys Ed? Why am *I* doing Phys Ed?

'On the next breath, straighten your spine slowly, vertebrae by vertebrae – and then you're going to let out that breath all at once.' He demonstrates, nimble as a yogi. 'Aaaaaaaaaaaah!' A singing yogi, apparently.

I must still be dreaming. Although I am at least at school this time, in my dream. Further down the row I can see Chloe and India 'aaaaaaaaaahing'. They clearly haven't realised that straightening your spine does not mean curving it backwards to thrust out your boobs. Or … yeah, maybe they have. Mr Battersby ignores them completely, which they find annoying.

Instead of gazing at them with deep admiration for their general perkiness, as they expect, he – oh, why does this keep happening? – slides over to me.

'Okay there, Sasha? We're straightening …' he says, showing me how to stand up, '… and ahhhhhhhhhhhh!'

I straighten quickly and let out my breath so fast that I shout in his face. 'Aghgh!'

Mr Battersby chews his lip for a moment, head on one side. I can't tell if he's trying not to laugh or is about to cry, but suddenly he nods. 'We'll work on it,' he announces to me. 'I hear the beginnings of something very interesting there.' He points at the upper part of my stomach. 'Stick it out more.'

'More?' mutters someone further down the gym. 'Is that possible?'

I guess that Suzette and Dana are also in the room, overarching their spines and aaaaaaaahing like backing singers.

Mr Battersby grimaces in their direction, then quickly smiles at me. 'Good breathing will sort the chorus from the stars, so don't neglect it,' he says before clapping his hands. Chorus from stars? I don't understand. This must be dream-language. Stars. It's night-speak. 'Form a circle! A circle around me, please.'

So we all shuffle into a ring as I try to retrace my steps mentally. Maybe I'm not asleep in my bed but have sleep-walked into school. I glance at the clock – yes, 7.45am. I was meant to meet Felix early, but somehow I've trotted past the office and the hall and the labs and the temporary classrooms, all the way to the gym. I just need to back away. Back gently out of the gym and backwards all the way to the school office. I look for the door to make my escape but it's closed. It'll squeak if I run and open it.

The circle has formed around Mr Battersby. It's a large circle, half the size of the gym – and it's all girls. There must be about two dozen of us from the top end of the school. Twenty of them look like the Swishers or actually are the Swishers.

The others are people I've never met before – a small dark girl with glasses, who's furiously reading the sheet of A4 paper she's clutching, mouthing words to herself; two girls in lycra who can't stop giggling and obviously just happened to be in the gym doing Olympic floor exercises with ribbons when the inhaling began, and me.

Swishers. Outliers.

Them. Us.

And Battersby knows it. 'You three,' he calls with a grin. 'Giggling Girls and Briony. Into the middle. Sasha, you come too.'

I have to speak around the heart that's lunged up my windpipe and into my mouth. 'Me?'

'Are there any other Sashas?'

I hope so. Please let there be another Sasha. I glance around the room, and there are no more Sashas. 'I'm meant to be … somewhere,' I squeak.

There are a few sniggers, but Mr Battersby outdoes them all by bursting, inexplicably, into song.

'Somewheeeeeeeeeerrre!' he bellows – although that's not fair, as he's got a beautiful voice and the word he sings sounds incredible. To my utter, utter and total horror, he suddenly clutches both my hands between his and carries on, directly into my face.

'There's a place for us.

A time and place for us.

Hold my hand and we're halfway there.

Hold my hand and I'll take you there.

Somehow! Someday! Somewhere!'

And I don't know if it's embarrassment or fear or I've actually just fallen completely in love with Mr Battersby - who I'm pretty sure is gay and touching forty anyway - or something else altogether, but as he cries 'Somewhere!' just above my head, his voice bouncing back off the climbing frames as he squeezes my fingers, I find tears rolling down my face.

I know that song. It's from my dad's favourite musical, West Side Story. Which is the musical the school put on for their annual production four or so months ago because Year 11 are doing 'Romeo and Juliet' and it sort of fits the curriculum while still being fun.

Which is when I work out where I am.

This is the audition.

The audition that I came to before school, one morning six or seven months ago. It was a morning I'd had to pre-arrange with George and Olivia so I could get out early;

when Felix had volunteered to come in with his mum so he could stop me backing out; when I'd promised myself that I'd give it a go.

Without even looking, I know that on the outside of that closed door is a notice saying, 'Girls' roles – Maria, Anita (leads); Consuelo, Rosalia, Anybodys, Velma, Graziella (speaking/dancing); Jet Girls/Ensemble/Chorus.'

I know exactly what it says, because I stood outside reading it for about eight minutes, hopping from one foot to other as I held down fear-vomit. I'd peered through the window at the girls already inside and seen who those girls were. Swishers, every one of them. I'd opened the door just the tiniest crack, trying to force myself to walk in. Felix had done his best to shove me through the door.

But in the end I couldn't. Couldn't make myself. Not even to make my dad proud – because he wasn't here any longer and he wouldn't get to see it anyway. Those incredible tunes and Shakespearean fights would be wasted without him there to experience them.

It didn't stop me being jealous when India got the lead role of Maria, even though she couldn't really act, and she kept looking directly at her parents in the audience. It didn't stop me regretting it, either – that I hadn't been brave enough. Because that was what it really boiled down to.

Mr Battersby drops my hands, spreading his own apart to create a little pathway to the centre of the circle. For me. For the only Sasha in the room. 'Still got to be somewhere?' he asks me quietly.

I gulp, hardly able to take it in. I'm back here again. It's like the sky-diving, only this is something I really wanted to do. I still want to do it. I'm getting another do-over, and even if it's a dream do-over I'd be insane not to take it.

Not quite believing what I'm doing (and I'm not the only one, judging by the expressions on the Swishers' faces), I nod to Mr Battersby. 'Yes,' I tell him. 'The middle of the circle.'

A tiny smile passes over his face. 'Good,' he says. 'Briony, please share the speech with Sasha, Ellie and ...'

'Shannon,' says the skinnier of the giggling girls, still giggling.

Briony gathers us round in her in a rugby huddle and shows us the speech. 'Go for it, all of you,' she whispers in her surprisingly firm voice. 'I've got no chance of getting a lead anyway.'

I glance at her quickly, recognising the voice – and instantly picture her in a police hat and uniform.

'Oh!' I cry. They all stare at me. 'But you are ... could be a lead. Officer Krupke – that's a big part! You'll be brilliant at it. Probably,' I add quickly when I realise I'm telling her fortune.

'Officer Krupke? That's a great part! But isn't he a man?'

I shrug. 'Just a police officer. Who says it has to be a male?'

Going by her expression, Briony does some quick mental calculation before thrusting the paper into my hand. 'Go on. You three share it. I know it off by heart anyway.'

Ellie and Shannon both flap their hands, batting it away as if it's infectious. 'No! No. You do it.' Ellie cracks up again. 'We're not even meant to be here. We just didn't leave fast enough!'

'I know that feeling,' I tell them, making them giggle again.

They're silly and bouncy and fun. Briony is clever and fun. I can already see her picturing herself as Krupke, twirling a truncheon as she goes about her duties. I don't know if she gets the part because I've suggested it, or does the part so that I know she'll get it, but somehow this weird circular moment has created a shift. These girls are great, non-Swisher types – the type of girls I could be friends with but have never seemed to connect with before.

'Right!' shouts Battersby.

Behind him, another little gaggle of girls stands in the centre of the circle. Three of the original Swishers have been joined by a Year 13 who looks like Wonder Woman. Even Chloe is a little in awe. Dana is staring daggers at her from her position in the circle, evidently less than impressed that she didn't get selected.

Briony suddenly snorts and digs me in the ribs. 'Look, we're like a Venn diagram of auditioners. The whole group, the beautiful girls,' she says with a nod at Wonder Woman and the Swishers, 'and the character parts. Otherwise known as us.'

I laugh, because it's true, but even as she says it I know that's not quite right, because Maria is both beautiful and a character part. The role at the intersection of all three groups. A strong female. A role to die for.

Or at least a role to audition for.

Mr Battersby calls us to attention by dropping his voice theatrically. 'It's dark,' he hisses. 'The boys have been fighting. Knives have been drawn – and used! And now there's a gun. People have died. People you love. Now you fight for them.' He ushers Chloe and co into the circle's very centre. 'You're Sharks. They're Jets. Go.'

For a second they all stare at him, then at us, as if he's been speaking in an alien language. It's the first time I've ever seen the Swishers not know what to do. Even Wonder Woman is poised to flee the circle.

But then Briony comes to life. 'Hey!' she yells, suddenly American. 'Are you kids fighting again?' She barges up to Wonder Woman and shoves her face right up at under her chin. 'I don't think you'd like a night behind bars, lady.'

Wonder Woman glares at her, suddenly fired up. 'Yeah? And who are you?' she shouts. It's not clear whether she's playing a part or genuinely doesn't know.

'Who am I?' Briony spins her invisible truncheon. 'I'm a police orrrrficer. Krupke is the name. All your boys know me well.'

India is frozen to the spot, but when Briony prods her in the arm she seems to shake herself into action, although she keeps checking whether her friends are watching. 'Well, it's a good job you're here, Officer, because those Jets are the ones who started it. Arrest them!'

'Arrest them? All of them?' yells Briony, and they all turn to see who "all of them" is. The whole room turns to see, caught up in the drama that Briony has inspired.

On either side of me, Ellie and Shannon are convulsed with nervous laughter. They're going to be no help at all – and suddenly it makes me mad. The whole thing makes me mad. People not helping when they should. Swishers looking me up and down when they're no better at this than I am. Police Officer Krupke threatening to arrest innocent people who are just trying to help their families … their dying family members …

I grab the script so hard that it rips in my hand as I run forward, straight in front of Briony and the Swishers and Wonder Woman. 'No!' I cry. 'Not all of them. Me. Arrest me!'

Krupke smirks. 'Why you, lady?'

I point at India, reading from the script for the first time.

"How many bullets are left, Chino? Enough for you?" I wave to Chloe – angry. So angry. 'And you?' There's so much anger in me that I spin around, sweeping up the whole circle with my fury. 'All of you? YOU ALL KILLED HIM! And my brother and Riff! Not with bullets and knives. WITH HATE! Well,' I whisper, my voice quiet because I'm sobbing, actually streaming with tears, 'I can hate too. Because now I HAVE HATE!'

I do too, pouring out of me like venom into the words and the gym and the faces of the onlookers who are all shocked and a little horrified to hear my voice hit the ceiling like Mr Battersby's, to see my face streaked with tear-stains and rage. Suddenly the energy leaks out of me. I drop the script to the floor. My weapon. Now I'm just me again. Crying.

It's only when Briony presses a tissue into my hand that I realise nobody has spoken yet. Ohhhh, this is so much worse than sky-diving. I've embarrassed myself and everyone here with my Liv-levels of hysterics.

'I'm sorry,' I blurt to Mr Battersby. 'I don't even know where that came from.'

He's crying too. Was I really that bad?

But then he runs over and lifts my arm in the air, like a prize fighter in the ring. 'Wherever it came from, you keep tapping into it. Maria, everyone! We've found our Maria! Oh, and our Office Krupke, I believe.'

There's hearty clapping from the smallest Venn diagram circle, echoed by a ripple of applause from the wider group, most of whom seem quite weirded-out. There's no noise from the Swisher circle, I notice.

But Battersby is shouting instructions as I stand there in a daze. 'Great, thank you, everyone! I'll list the other parts by lunchtime, and anyone who was brave enough to audition deserves at least a part in the chorus. We need lots of dancers.'

Shannon and Ellie high-five. 'Yay!'

'You're in it!' I cry, pleased for them.

'You too!' they chorus.

I'm not just in it. I'm Maria. I've got to sing, and dance, and act, and remember lines, and … kiss! I'm going to have to kiss Tony!

'Mr Battersby,' I cry, stumbling after him as he pushes auditioners out of the room. 'Have you found Tony yet?'

'Oh! Yes, good question.' He beams at me, knowing what my concerns are. 'Don't worry, you won't mind the love scenes. Very good-looking lad. Amazing singer. We're so lucky he's arrived at the school just at the right time. Actually, he even suggested you for Maria.' He smiles again, delighted with his finds. 'You'll meet him soon. His name is—'

I don't even need to hear it to know who it will be.

'… Cass Ely.'

Chapter 7 Cass-time

Breathe in, breathe out, and keep doing it, I tell myself. And again. I fully expect the school to disappear as soon as I step outside the gym. I'll wake up, a string of spittle cascading from the corner of my mouth, and probably with a whole theatrical circle of people around me to witness the drool.

But I don't. Instead I stare at the sheet of paper I knew would be there and see the name of the part I've just got at the top of the list.

Maria. I'm Maria. Mariaaaaaaaa. I just met a girl called Mariaaaaa. And suddenly I imagine Cass Ely singing that song, as he will have to as Tony, and shake my head in amazement.

'Why are you so red?' says a voice from the shadows.

Felix stares as I clutch my cheeks. They are burning ridiculous amounts. 'Exercise,' I say quickly. 'I mean, breathing exercises for singing. From the diaphragm and all that.'

He seems to believe me. 'So? Did you do it?'

I want to laugh, it's so unfathomable. 'I didn't just do it, Felix,' I say, blushing scarlet again. 'I aced it.'

One eyebrow lifts. 'Seriously?'

I point to the name 'Maria' on the list, and then at myself.

'You got the MAIN PART?' he yells in disbelief, just as Chloe and team swing through the gym door.

'Of course she didn't,' says Suzette. 'India's going to get it.'

'You are, India,' confirms Chloe, as if it's all down to her.

But he said it … Mr Battersby said it was me. I gulp, wondering suddenly if I've imagined it. I am asleep, after all.

Then the man himself steps up behind us all. 'Don't block the doorways,' he commands, back in teacher mode instead of Broadway star mode. 'And don't tell lies, Suzette. You all heard me tell Sasha that she's Maria.'

Suzette glares at me. 'I assumed you were joking, Mr Battersby,' she says with a sniff. 'You also said that short girl would be playing a policeman. Joking, yes?'

'Police officer. I said Briony would be a police officer. And Maria is going to be played by Sasha. As I said.' He points to the notice. 'But India, you did do well. Would you like to be Anyones?'

Felix can't help himself. He snorts in a way that says, "she already is."

India is practically purple with rage at the thought of being anyone but Maria. 'I don't play bit parts.'

'Ah, okay,' says Mr Battersby. 'I'll remember that.'

He's about to walk off when India grabs his arm. 'So who am I playing?'

The air is thick with something a little unpleasant. She's just waiting. They're all waiting – for Mr B to tell us he's got it all wrong, and of course India is in the lead role. But he doesn't.

He shrugs. 'Well, there's not much option if you'll only play the lead. You have to be a team player to be a cast member, India. Maybe think about that for your next audition.'

'You mean I'm not in it?' She gasps, turning to the others. 'I'm not in it!'

Six mouths drop open, including mine and my friend's. If Felix and I can hardly believe that she's done herself out of a role altogether, the Swishers look like they're ready to kill someone.

'My dad will hear about this,' says Chloe. 'He's a lawyer.'

Mr Battersby puts his head on one side. 'Lucky we hadn't signed contracts then, isn't it? Now, class is about to st—'

'Anyway, don't worry, Inds,' blurts Dana loudly. 'I bet the male lead is a total dud. He must be if we haven't heard of him. Sasha will have to smooch some ugly dude on stage in front of everyone.'

Then a voice rings out from the top of the stairs. 'You got the part then, Sash?'

71

Honestly, he's backlit by the hall's fluorescent tubes. Practically shining.

'Who is *that*?' the girls all squeak amongst themselves, hands fluttering to their hair, cleavage, skirt-shortening waistband.

I spit his name out under my breath. 'Cass Ely.'

'It's … that's Tony? That GUY is TONY?' cries India, even more incensed. 'You'll get to kiss HIM?'

And it's only when she punches me hard in the arm and I experience pain – real, gonna bruise levels of pain – that I realise a whole host of horrible truths.

They don't know who he is. Even Felix is gawping at him like he can't believe his eyes.

This really is six months before, and it really is school, and I really have just landed a major part in the school production. And the male lead is Cass bloody Ely who is doing everything he can to make my life as unbearable and dangerous as possible, when it's already pretty unbearable a lot of the time.

'Don't Sash me,' I cry up the stairs, rubbing my arm as India stares at it and then at Mr Battersby, a tiny bit horrified at herself.

The teacher mouths one word at her, and my disastrous fate is sealed. 'Detention.'

'No!' I cry. 'She didn't mean it, did you, India? She was high-fiving me, weren't you, India?'

'No, I meant it,' she says bitterly. 'Suck-up. Don't think you'll be friends with us now, Baker, just because you're the star of the show.'

'I … I didn't …'

I really didn't, because I can't imagine anything worse than having four beautiful friends who not-so-secretly hate you. It's not like I have masses of alternatives or anything, but nothing would make me pretend to like them just to be "in".

Cass Ely, meanwhile, is making his way down the stairs towards me. Any second now he's going to propose to me or something, and then I'll be horribly dead.

I'm just wondering how to get out of this new dilemma when I'm saved by an unlikely source.

'Sasha!' giggles Ellie, running past him down the stairs. 'I've totally got your bag instead of mine! I'm such an idiot.' She holds my backpack up over Felix's head. 'This is yours, right?'

'Yes.' Keep it brief, Sasha. Don't say anything else that can possibly be taken the wrong way.

'Mine must still be in the gym. Can I go back in, Mr B?'

The teacher grins and blocks the door. 'Only if you and Shannon agree to be in the chorus.'

Ellie squeals in delight. 'You weren't kidding? I can't believe it! We're in the play? Wow!'

The Swishers lose interest fast now that the focus isn't on them. Checking out Cass on the way as if they're faintly disgusted by his beauteous presence, they stalk off to lessons, leaving the me and the two guys grouped on the stairs up from the gym. Ellie blusters back through the door with her bag, still laughing.

'I can't believe it. Wait until I tell Shannon! She'll wet herself!'

'Perhaps you shouldn't tell her then,' says Cass Ely, a little worried for the first time since we met six months … ahead.

Ellie screeches with laughter. 'Not really! At least I hope not! Come on, Sasha. Let's go and find her to give her the good news.'

'Can we come?' wails Felix like a six-year-old. I can't tell if he's pretending.

'Sure,' says Ellie easily, although she doesn't look at all bothered whether they join us or not and hasn't even paused long enough to be mesmerised by yellow-green eyes and a powerful nose.

And now that I glance at them again, the eyes are more hazel than yellow, and the nose more long than beaky, and suddenly he's not terrifyingly gorgeous. Pretty lush, for sure, but in a more approachable way.

'So why are you here?' I ask him as we follow the blur that is Ellie along the corridor, Felix stumbling slightly as he tries to keep up.

The eyes glance down at me. 'Why are any of us here? Curiosity, I suppose you'd call it.'

'You're at this school because of curiosity?' Weird. 'Not because … your parents just moved house or you can't do drama at your school?'

'Oh. Yes. Both of those,' he says quickly, so I know he's lying.

I test him out. 'So what school were you at before?'

'This big academy,' he says, stretching his arms out and cracking his knuckles. 'You won't have heard of it.'

Felix turns around. 'Sash, we'll be late for English. You coming?' he calls, just as Ellie spots Shannon and races over, gangly legs whirling as she screams: 'We're in! We're really in! Sash, over here! You too, Eyebrows.'

And we all jump up and down in excitement, high-fiving and laughing, even Felix, before agreeing to catch up to chat about the Swishers' reaction over lunch, and they'll grab Briony too, and Cass says he'll join us to everyone's amazement …

I half-smile all the way through English and German. I'm Maria. I'm Maria and I've got friends. I've got a group. Not the populars – but not the nerds either. Just … the Normals doing drama. Or at least, they would be the Normals if the group didn't include Cass Ely.

But the more normal we are with him, the more normal he seems to me. He's nice. He's kind. They all are, but Cass is especially good to me. And it's about time something or someone other than Felix, his mother and my own family was good to me.

I see them all across the cafeteria, gathered round a table. He's sitting at the head of the long rectangle, listening to something Briony is saying with a slight frown on his hawky face. He raises a hand as I approach, and they all turn to wave me over, grinning, laughing, apart from Felix who appears to be having extra eyebrow trouble as he glances around the table, from me to Cass and back again …

Then Cass stands and gives me his seat and a feeling like I've never known floods over me. I can't really describe it, and the only thing close to it is the moment I just had with Mr Battersby. Eugh. I mean, not with Mr Battersby, but in that beautiful soaring musical connection when he sang 'Somewhere' to me.

Cherished. I feel cherished.

I smile gratefully at Cass Ely as I take his seat … and then I keep going … and going … and going …

The grin is wiped off my face when my butt makes contact with the cafeteria floor.

'Oh, sorry, Sasha,' says Chloe, not sounding sorry at all, in fact, hardly able to keep the smirk off her face. 'I didn't realise that seat was taken.'

'Wow,' says Briony in her deep, cutting voice. 'You didn't see a whole person about to sit down on a chair that had someone else on it just seconds before. You really must be as dumb as you look.'

Chloe swivels around as if she'd been stung. She bends down and thrusts her face into Briony's. 'Did you just call me stupid?'

'Just speculating,' says Briony with a shrug.

Meanwhile Ellie and Felix are peeling me off the floor. My back hurts. There's a chance I've detached some vertebrae. I know a lot about spines and bones and joints, with Mum's illness and everything, and slipping a disk or two with everything I've got on could be terrible.

'Leave it, Chloe,' says one of her friends. I'm surprised to see it's India. 'She's not worth it. He only gave her the part because he felt sorry for her. Don't bother trying to get even.'

Cass is watching the whole monologue with his hands on his hips. Say something, Cherisher, I plead with him silently. Stand up for me.

I'm sure he's just about to say something … pretty sure, anyway … when Felix steps in between me and Chloe.

'Haven't you got enough?' He points to India and then Chloe. 'Haven't you been blessed enough with your rich parents and your orthodontists and tutors and expensive hairdressers? Can't you let someone else have some of the limelight when they deserve it?'

India flushes uncomfortably, but Chloe's having none of it. 'Why does Sasha deserve it? Because she's fat and we should feel sorry for her?'

'She's not—'

'Sasha totally nailed that audition—'

'Yes, you should feel sorry for her!'

They all shout at once, jumping to my defence, but I tune in quickly to what Felix is saying. Yes. You should feel sorry for her.

'You don't know what she's been through,' he's saying. 'What she goes through every day.'

'And what's that?' snarls Chloe. 'The McDonalds drive-through?'

Felix's bottom lip curls away from his teeth in as vicious a snarl as I've ever seen. 'If you weren't a girl…' he hisses.

He'd punch her. I see where this is going. He'd slap her, and then they'd hate me even more, and they might even find out about Mum and everything at home because she'd get called to the office.

It's not worth it, I think. I just got carried away. I can't manage rehearsals and practices anyway, unless they're in the school lunch hour, and some of them are bound to be after school when I'm meant to be Other Me, At-Home Sasha.

Cass Ely is still standing watching, like some kind of sports referee. I won't get to kiss you, I think sadly.

Then I say what the Swishers want to hear, to avoid the things I don't want to hear.

'It's fine. It's not worth it. I'll pull out, and then Maria will be free and you can do it, India.'

She bridles at me. 'You think I want your leftovers, Fatty Baker?'

I have to swallow hard at that one, laying a hand on Felix's sleeve so he doesn't deck her, girl or not. 'The role should be yours. I'm okay at the singing but ... you're a better all-rounder. You look the part.'

She stares at me, not sure whether to be pleased or offended. A wave of disappointment wafts off my new friends. 'Well, if you're sure,' says India finally, victory making her fake-pleasant.

'I'll tell Mr Battersby,' I confirm. 'And India – don't look at the audience when you're on stage.'

'As if,' she says, outraged. And of course I can't explain. I'm just trying to help.

I walk away, tears threatening to stream down my face where I don't brush them away with the back of my hand. Nobody follows me. I think they all know I need to be on my own.

I don't even bother telling Mr Battersby, because I know that this do-over hasn't worked. I'll wake up at some point, and it will just be as if it never happened.

I go home, cry a little, make tea for everyone as if it's been a perfectly average day. Then I go to bed, aware that when I wake up in the morning, it'll be back to normal.

India will kiss Cass as he sings 'Somewhere' to her.

Swishers will win out over Normals.

And Sasha Baker will just be living her usual, terrible vie.

Chapter 8 Back to BB

Breathe right down past your ribs, I tell myself to confirm that I'm okay. Right down your spine, Sasha. See if your back's broken. No? You're fine. Still alive, at least. My chest rises and falls with oxygen, easy and steady.

I've woken early in the morning, before the birds start warbling. *Did* I dream it all? It feels like the usual start to the day, with Mum struggling to do her exercises from the edge of her bed in the room next door, and Olivia shout-snorting across the landing, sort of shneerrp-AAAAGH!, just as she always does just before she wakes herself up with her own snoring. Loud. All the time, loud. I'm already on alert for her singing in the shower as if she's on The Voice.

And that reminds me of a way to check whether this is a school day after an episode in which I've got myself into enormous poop with the Swishers and possibly Mr B, or a Body Beautiful day. Throwing back the duvet, then automatically straightening it to save myself a job later, I scramble over to my desk on all fours. Where did I put it?

It's hiding between my Year 11 copy of Hamlet, saved just because I love it, and a stack of magazines that I've confiscated from Olivia because she started to use words like 'body image' and 'thigh gap'.

WEST SIDE STORY, by Peterview Comprehensive. The date is from the previous term.

It happened. I went to the performance and watched India play the whole thing to her parents and wished it could have been me. Well, it *could* have been me, if only I'd been braver and/or more of an ordinary teenager. I think of India pashing Cass on stage, several times in a week, and my stomach clenches a little. Maybe that was why I'd recognised him! He was the lead in my dad's favourite musical and India got to snog him, making me jealous on two or three different fronts. Of course. Turning the page, I glance down the cast list. Maria … India Cleverley. Tony …

I grab the page and peer at it more closely. Not Cass Ely. Todd Minchin. Handsome Todd Minchin from Year 13, who could actually sing and actually act. He was so professional he'd almost made India look good at it. The picture shows him in rehearsal, belting out "Maria" to the back of the hall with a dreamy look in his eyes. And now I remember that I hadn't been jealous at all, because he may be handsome and starry but he's also a jock and completely full of himself.

So where was Cass? I scan through all the photos in the programme – but there's no sign of him at all. He must have dropped out of the production too – or I'd imagined the whole thing.

'Saaaaaaash!' Olivia suddenly screams, right outside my door. 'It's seven am. Why aren't you up?'

'I am up!'

'You stole my mindfulness book! I've got to take it today,' she bellows.

I open the door and speak in a normal voice, which is all that's necessary given we're standing half a metre apart. 'I borrowed it. Here you go.'

I'm about to hand her the programme instead, but then notice my mistake and snatch the textbook from my bedside table. 'There.'

She sighs. 'Are you still wishing you'd auditioned for that play? Honestly, Sasha. It's gone. Forget about it. That's mindfulness – live in the present.'

And she's right. So, so right. I nod. 'I know. I was just doing some recycling.'

'Not my magazines!' she shrieks. 'I need them!'

I open the door and shove her towards the bathroom. 'You do not. What you need is a shower.'

She screams again, horrified at the thought that she might smell or have non-shiny hair or commit some other social crime at school with her new evil besties. 'Get me out in ten minutes!'

'Five. Mum needs the bathroom,' I remind her.

'O-kayyyyyy!' That's her "stop nagging me" voice, as if I've been on about it for hours.

She whisks away in her normal tornado, and I stare at the bathroom door as she slams it behind her. How did I end up here, forcing my little sister to shower instead of starring in dreamy musicals?

And then I remember how. Dad. Mum. Stuff.

It's time for Mum to get up, so I push open her bedroom door. 'Morning, Mum. You awake?'

'Are you kidding? All the drugs in the world wouldn't let me sleep through that ruckus.'

'What if we drugged Liv instead?' I suggest.

Mum laughs, but it hurts her this morning. I help her sit up, and we get on with it all.

Having to be extra careful with Mum and give additional instructions to George slows me down a little, so as predicted, I'm a tiny bit late for The Body Beautiful. It doesn't seem to matter though: Charlotte is still in her jeans and super-tight t-shirt, leaning on the high reception desk as she chats to the woman behind it.

'So I told him we do male eyebrows. I mean, I know we haven't done many so far, but we should totally do it as a special. I've booked in for –' She turns as I walk in, caramel hair swinging across her cheek. 'Sasha, hi! Annette, this is Sasha, on wonderful work experience.'

The woman looks up from the computer screen with a smile that doesn't match the worried look in her eyes.

'Hello, Sasha. So sorry I wasn't around to meet you when you came in before.'

'No problem,' I say, as it really wasn't. I lay down on your bed and fell asleep. Maybe I should be the one to apologise.

'Did Charlotte show you around?' She glances at Charlotte for confirmation and notices her jeans, the untied hair. 'Oh, Charlie! Uniform!'

Charlotte looks down at herself. 'Derr. Sorry. Completely forgot. Though we've got one for you, too, Sasha – haven't we, Auntie Nets?'

"Auntie Nets" grins at my confused expression. 'Yep, it's a family business. Otherwise I'd never have gone someone as talented as Charlotte to work for me for minimum wage.' Charlotte rolls her eyes prettily as Annette continues. "I'm sorry to say that's why we leapt at the chance of someone on work experience too. Are you sure you don't mind being free labour? We can pay you in treatments!'

'Treatments?' I'm so excited I shout it across the reception area. 'That's way better than money! Not that I expected money anyway. Just … you know, work. And experience.'

Annette and Charlotte laugh together, the family resemblance showing all over their tanned and glowy faces. 'Work we can give you,' says Annette, 'though it's not going to be very glamorous, I'm afraid. I can send you on some work trips, though.'

'You can?'

She grins again, her teeth blindingly white. 'Oh yes. The laundrette is way over in the next street, and we need someone doing very regular visits to the supermarket for chocolate.'

I can't help but smile back at them both. Nice, beautiful people who even scoff chocolate. 'This is going to be the best work experience ever!' I declare, and they high-five each other as if I've given them an award.

'Okay, ladies, work gear on. Let's get ready for all our customers!' cries Annette.

Once again, the two of them chuckle madly; for a moment I wonder if they're a bit nuts. Maybe the treatment chemicals have affected them.

But then Charlotte says, 'You'll see, Sasha,' and I figure that it's not the pair of them who are odd, but possibly the customers.

While Charlotte disappears into the bigger treatment room to get changed, Annette passes me something wrapped in shiny plastic and points to the door to the room I'd slept in. 'Try it for comfort,' she says. 'We can always swap it if it's not right.'

Size. She didn't say size. In fact, now that she's stepped out from behind the counter I see that she's also curvy, not skinny, but very well turned out with a slight sway to her walk that makes her move silently and rather slinkily. There's a word for it – sashay. Annette sashays. She grins at me again and closes the door as I inspect the package in my hands.

My uniform turns out to be black leggings with a slight boot-leg, and a matching black tunic that crosses over, loops round my waist and ties at the side. Around the edge, it's piped with pale green – the same pale green as the window – and it bears a tiny badge saying 'Body Beautiful' in curved lettering. To my relief, it covers me from head to toe apart from a small triangle at my neck and my arms, without any bulging or gapping or sticking to my jiggling back. When I catch sight of myself in the mirror on the back of the door, I'm amazed to find that it actually looks … nice.

'Wow,' says Annette as I walk back into Reception. 'You should wear black more often.'

'Oh my life, Sasha.' Charlotte fake-groans. 'You're not meant to look better than me. Are you after my job on Reception?'

I'm still shaking my head, not quite sure if she's joking despite the big grin on her face, when the door opens.

Charlotte jumps out of her orange skin. 'All my days, a customer!' she exclaims, manicured hand on her chest as she pants with the shock of it all.

Annette stares at her, trying not to smile, then turns to the door. 'Please ignore my colleague. She's not had her coffee yet. How can we help?'

'We're doing men's eyebrows! Boys, I mean. Young men's!' blurts Charlotte, before covering her own mouth in shame at speaking out of turn. She's blushing so deeply beneath her spray tan that she looks newly sunburnt.

I'm so busy watching them that I haven't even looked at the customer yet.

'Well,' he says carefully, 'I think my eyebrows are fine, but do you do young men's fingernails?'

Cass Ely. Cass Beautiful Ely, getting his nails done in my salon.

He's getting annoying.

'Why do you need your nails done? You?' I snap, before Annette can even respond.

Cass holds out his hands. His nails could slice bread. 'I'm going to be working at SkyDivers,' he explains to Charlotte and Annette, who are both trying so hard not to stare at his beaky gorgeousness that they're a little cross-eyed.

'Well, those nails won't do with all that parachute silk around,' says Annette with a nod.

'And I'm on Reception,' he adds.

'I'm on Reception!' cries Charlotte happily. 'You definitely need nice nails.'

'Great,' he says. 'So when can you fit me in? I start in an hour.'

'Now!' they shout together.

There's a small scuffle as they both try to lead him to the nail desk in the corner of the Reception area. Charlotte wins.

As if Annette suddenly realises how it must look with them scrapping over a guy half her age, she suddenly nods briskly. 'I'll leave you in Charlotte's capable hands. Sasha, let's get you doing some tasks, shall we?' She walks off to the treatment rooms.

'I'll just get my equipment,' breathes Charlotte.

For a second I'm left alone with Cass Ely. He gazes evenly at me as I try to figure out where to start with having a go at him. It's quite possible the whole musical thing was just a dream, even though it felt so completely and utterly real. Not there then. I could ask what he's doing here – here, in this place where he knew I'd be working – but his nails really do need sorting out. Just by waving casually at someone, he could rip life-saving equipment to shreds. He's got a perfectly legitimate reason for being at The Body Beautiful.

I've now been looking into his eyes for a good few long moments while I try to figure it out. His pupils are growing hypnotically – or at least that's what I think until I realise it's my own reflection in them as I draw closer and closer to him.

'You look good in black,' he says, at the same moment as I snap: 'Were you in my garden last night?'

'Thanks.' I squirm self-consciously, wondering if I should repeat myself.

'Sorry, I didn't catch that. Was I …'

Obviously I should have repeated myself. I'm just about to when Charlotte and her aunt appear in the doorway. 'Sorry, had to find the big clippers,' says Charlotte. 'Been so long since we had a customer for a manicure.' She corrects herself quickly. 'A male customer.'

Annette smiles at me. 'I'm so used to Charlotte knowing her way around, I probably didn't tell you to follow me in here, did I? My apologies, Sasha. You'll get used to us!'

The space between me and Cass has now been filled by Charlotte. The moment has gone. 'Good luck with SkyDivers,' I say instead.

'I'd wish you the same for here,' he replies, 'but you obviously won't need any luck. What a lovely placement you've landed, Sasha Baker.'

He winks a solemn yellow-green eye at Charlotte, and she practically chops the end of his finger off with the man-sized nail clippers. If people could genuinely have emoji hearts beating out of their eyes like Tom and Jerry or Tik-Tok, she would have them now. They've bonded over twin reception duties and general gorgeousness, and by the looks of it, Charlotte has fallen head-over-pumice-stoned-heels in love.

For some reason, it doesn't bother me in the same way as it did when it was India. Although that was just a dream, so maybe it wouldn't really bother me at all if she and Cass became an item. My stomach cramps up but I ignore it. No. India and Cass together would bother me. But Cass and Charlotte? She's so nice that maybe she deserves him – and he can't actually be interested in me anyway …

I spend the next half hour having my eyelashes tinted as Annette experiments with a new lash treatment and tells me all about the business. Not going well. Thought Charlotte would help in sales by doing all the social media stuff, but Charlotte's shy and hates it. Will I do it? Also shy and hate it, I tell her. Also not really wanting anyone to find out more about my life, I don't tell her. Annette goes on. Might have to close down if sales don't improve. Cass has been their first paying customer this week. I offer to pay for my eyelashes and she wafts the dye wand at me. No, no. This is your work experience. You're helping us.

I really don't see how, although I suppose it was my presence that brought in Cass. I'm really hoping he's planning to pay. Then as Annette starts on my eyebrows (just to make them match up to my fabulous lashes) I think that it's obvious why they're not making any money. They're so nice that everyone likes them. Everyone's a friend. And you don't charge friends …

Charlotte runs in with the hand towel she'd laid under Cass's fingers. She clutches it to her cheek. 'I may never wash it! Oh, Sasha, so sorry if you and Cass are together. You lucky thing.'

'We're not together,' I tell her, wondering how she could ever imagine that would be possible.

'Ohhhhh!' she croons, sucking in the towel scent.

Annette whips it out of her hand and passes it to me. 'Sorry, my darling niece. He may be the love of your life, but that towel needs washing. Health and Safety.'

'Ohhhhhh!' Charlotte sighs. She shrugs. 'It's okay, though. He's coming back next week for a pedicure.'

'Did he pay you?' I ask suddenly.

Charlotte nods. 'For today, and in advance for next week!'

The expression of hope in both their eyes is too unbearable, so I hold up the towel and repeat what Annette has told me. 'Small towels in the washer-dryer?'

'End of the corridor,' says Annette. 'Do you need help with the washer?'

But I know my way around a laundry. I find another mound of small red towels awaiting washing and pile them into the basket before feeding them one by one into the machine – and lucky that I do, as the towel Cass used has something stuck to it. I hold it up to the light. It's a very short quill – one of those pens used in Shakespearean times, made from a feather and sharpened at one end. I only know what they are because my dad used to like calligraphy.

Cass Ely is a very strange guy indeed. Who uses quills these days?

Then I wonder again why he came in. Was it to make me feel comfortable? Or maybe Charlotte? Perhaps he'd seen her the previous time I was in here and wanted to meet her in person. As I pour powder into the dispenser, I think of how happy Annette has been to be paid, how thrilled Charlotte has been to sit holding Cass's taloned fingertips.

I switch on the washing machine, and it's as if something in my brain switches too.

It's time to stop being so suspicious of Cass. Of everyone, really. And it's definitely time to stop dreaming about him. I hear the water pour into the drum, cleaning not just towels. Suddenly, somehow, my heart feels a little clearer too.

Chapter 9 Felix time

Breathe yourself clean." That's one of the messages of Liv's mindfulness book.

I take it seriously and try some "deep, cleansing breaths" before bed, and it seems to work. That night there are no dreams and no surprises, apart from a message to meet Felix early at the school office before heading into Work Experience, seeing as I hadn't shown at all that day. I text George and ask her if she can arrive an hour earlier, and luckily she can.

'Early morning date?' she says when she arrives at 7.15am the next day. Her nudge is so unsubtle it nearly propels me back down the hallway.

'Of course not. I'm meeting Felix.'

She glances behind her down the pathway. 'Oh, not – I thought … Anyway. How was the beauticians?'

I love George. She's so busy looking after so many people, and yet she can always remember just what you were last talking about and jump into questions as if she genuinely cares about the answer. Mum says it's what makes her the best carer in the world, because she hears the same thing every day for years and always acts like it's something new and fascinating.

Although in this case, it actually is new and fascinating.

'It's really lovely, and they're such nice people,' I tell her as I help her carry her various bags into the lounge. 'But I think they're struggling for business. Annette says they might have to close down.'

George raises her eyebrows. They're almost as big as Felix's eyebrows, I notice, and I wonder about getting her a gift certificate. 'That's no good,' she says. 'They're the only beauticians in town apart from that schmancy spa in the hotel. What kind of thing do they do?'

'Eyebrows,' I say casually, deliberately not looking at hers. 'Eyelashes. Manicures and pedicures for men and women. They've got beds out the back so I'm guessing they do massages as well.' I feel guilty for not knowing more about it.

George starts up the stairs to help Mum out of bed. 'I'll mention it to the other caregivers. Actually …' She pauses. 'We've got an office party coming up. Do they do off-site events? I'm sure some of the guys and gals would like a bit of pampering.'

'I don't know. I'll ask – and bring home some leaflets.'

'Great.' George nods upstairs. 'How's madam this morning?'

'Mum's fine, I think.'

'I meant Olivia.'

'Oh. Yeah, would you mind shoving her out of the door in ten minutes? She's supposed to be at school early for choir practice this morning.'

'My pleasure,' says George with a wink. 'I'm good at shoving. It's part of my job description.'

That's actually true, so we both laugh. I shout goodbye up to Mum and Liv, wave quickly to George and then head down the wheelchair ramp to the front gate.

It's still early; not quite light and with faint tendrils of mist curling across the pavements. The streets seem eery and a little sinister when they're like this at night - a bit Jekyll and Hydey - but when it's like this in the early morning, it always feels to me as if something precious is being born. I don't get to see it often, so I enjoy the easy pace of the stroll to the bus which deposits me near the school gates just before 8am.

Felix is hunched over the computer at the back of the school office, huddled into his jumper with his legs coiled beneath the chair.

'Are you cold?' I ask him.

'I'm making myself as small as possible so that I can't be seen and sent to class.'

'You are allowed to be here,' I point out. 'It's your work experience.'

He scowls. 'I'm making myself as small as possible so that I can't be seen and made to do work experience. Anyway,' he says, scooting around the desk in his wheely chair so he's right in front of me, 'how was the Body Beautiful?'

I perch on the edge of his mum's desk. 'Really, really good. They're lovely.'

'Well, Charlotte was very nice so I'm not surprised.'

Ah. So that's why he's asking how it all was. Charlotte. I try to let him down gently, but there's no easy way around it. 'Sorry, Felix. I think she's into Cass Ely.'

Felix's cheekbones change colour. 'When … how … what's he got to do with anything?'

'He came in yesterday for a manicure.'

'A manicure?' he shouts. 'Cass Ely had a manicure?'

I hold up my palms. 'Don't blame me. I didn't invite him.'

'But he came anyway?' He's unusually irritated by Cass Ely, I've noticed. Most people can make him a bit tetchy, but Cass really winds him up.

Felix stands up. 'So I suppose you all just stood around admiring him, did you? While some of us were—'

'I wasn't admiring him,' I said abruptly. 'I was in the back with the owner, Annette.'

'Doing what?'

I blush. 'Well, actually getting my eyelashes tinted, but also talking about work.'

'I knew you looked different,' snaps Felix. I wait for him to say "in a good way" but he doesn't. 'So you were having your make-up done while some of us were—'

'Not make-up. Eyelashes. And I did some work as well – washing and cleaning and all that. And they're actually in trouble, Felix.'

95

He scowls at me again. 'Well, you're actually in trouble, too.'

'I am?' I can't quite understand what's gone on here. I've made some innocent comments about what someone else is fully entitled to do, and somehow I'm at fault and Felix is cross with me. 'Why? Because of my eyelashes?'

'No!' yells Felix, jumping to his feet. 'Because of your genetics! You've been having all this fun with your quote unquote "new friends", while some of us were looking up your mum's disease and seeing if it can be passed on through the family! And the bad news is – it can!'

He crosses his arms in a huff, completely mad with me for some reason I can't work out, as if it's my own fault I've got my actual mother's DNA - but suddenly I can't worry about what Felix is annoyed at. I plop down into the seat he's just vacated.

'It's … it's genetic?' I whisper.

Felix takes my place at the edge of the desk, deflated like a popped balloon. 'Not exactly. Not in a way that can be passed on, mother to child. But there is a gene that can make you suspect … suspectable …'

'Susceptible,' I say, my voice hollow and hard.

Felix nods. 'Yeah, that. There about 200 genes that put you at greater risk of developing MS.' He swallows, and I think how hard that simple action has become for Mum lately. 'I think you can be tested, if that's any help.'

I can't even look at him. 'Why would it help?'

'You … you could be prepared?' he says tentatively.

'I can't! I can't be prepared!' I screech, startling Felix who's barely ever heard me say boo, let alone bark at someone. 'I just can't get it, okay? Who'd look after everyone? Who?'

And then I start to cry, which just about finishes him off. 'Don't. Don't, Sash. Look, I shouldn't have told you.'

'So why did you?'

'Because you asked me to. And because … because I didn't want to do all the worrying myself.'

'Yourself? You didn't want to worry?' For some reason this makes me incredibly, shudderingly mad with him, even though somewhere in my brain that is not yet affected by a debilitating disease I know it's unfair. 'Well, okay then! Don't bother! I'll just do all the worrying. All the worrying for everyone!'

'Sasha?' says someone in the doorway. It's Felix's mum, Mrs Webb. 'Are you all right?'

I push past her, not even able to shake my head, not wanting her to see my tears. Behind me I hear her ask Felix what he's done, and his sharp response: 'I *hate* Work Experience Week!'

I hate it too, I tell myself as I stomp down the pathway, back towards town. It's later now, so people are starting to drift into school. Several of the younger kids from the lower years stare at me as I stumble past them. I'm glad of my tinted eyelashes because mascara, if I ever wore it, would be streaking across my face like a dirty river bed right now. The older kids know better than to look, because looking might mean having to do something about it, so people either watch me blubbing with open mouths like I'm a circus act or pretend I'm invisible.

I'm just about able to withstand it until I realise that there are some bigger kids – my height, in fact, or certainly my year – who are neither gawking at me with gob-smacked expressions or avoiding my eye. They're actually looking straight at me, boldly, harshly even. One of them is actually smirking. They're also blocking the pavement in a little line of four, for all the world as if they're about to break into a bout of Irish dancing.

Swishers.

I try to go round them, prepared to fling myself under a car rather than push through the barrier of Chloe, India, Dana and Suzette, but Dana catches hold of my shoulder.

'Slow up there, perky pony,' she says flatly. The others snigger. I'm guessing they like the comparison to a large beast of burden that is anything but perky.

My mind's not at its clearest and I suddenly wonder if this is about the role of Maria. Is India still mad at me for that, even though I let her have it? But of course she can't be, because that didn't really happen. I have photographic proof that India played Maria opposite handsome Todd Minchin.

Suzette puts her head on one side. 'Work Experience not going well?' She has the nerve to sound a little sympathetic. 'Not surprising, given where you are.'

'No, it's … it's fine.'

It's something else, I want to say, because they're human and they must get that people have other things going on in their lives besides what they see directly in front of them … But I've set them off again.

'I bet it is.' India thrusts her face into mine and stares at me. 'Holy moley, have you had extensions?'

'Extensions?' I grab the end of my hair, and they all laugh. 'Oh, you mean eyelash extensions. No, they're just tinted.'

India sneers. 'So you get to hang out in a beauty shop having eyelash tints and flirting with new boys? Wish I'd been late to Work Experience Day!'

They all laugh again, nastily, as it dawns on me what they're on about. 'I didn't … you mean Cass Ely? I didn't flirt with him.'

Suzette folds her arms, smug as anything. 'Well, I saw him go into that store and the two of you were looking very cosy together.'

Every one of them is watching my face, waiting for me to trip myself up, to give myself away. Suddenly I'm sick of it. I've just had more terrible news about my already terrible vie and they think I even care about flirting with Mr Golden Eyes?

'Look, what do you want?' I say, straightening up. 'I've got to get to work.'

'We want you to stay away from Cass Ely,' says Suzette. 'One of us has a very special interest in him, and you'd do well not to get in the way.'

I look from one to the other of them. 'I wouldn't get in India's way,' I say carefully, 'but I think Cass may be interested in someone else anyway. Not me. Someone else. Someone nice.'

It's the wrong thing to say. I don't mean it to come out like that – as if they're not nice – but I hear it as it's coming out of my mouth and understand immediately that I've just fouled up in a major way.

'It's not India, Sasha,' says Chloe, doing the ultimate swish to one side. 'India's been going out with Todd Minchin since the play, which you'd know if you were anybody in this school.'

'It doesn't matter—' I start to say, but Chloe holds up a finger.

'It's me. I'm the one who's interested in Cass Ely. And I …' She skewers the finger into my cheek. '… am nice.'

There's a vast, awful moment where eyes twitch in the direction of Chloe's finger – a recognition that she's gone too far, even amongst her friends, which they daren't comment on, and a split second where they wonder if I'm going to retaliate. Where I wonder myself, in fact, if I'm going to retaliate …

I decide not to. Instead I back away from Chloe's fingernail, not meeting her eye or anyone else's. I pick up my bag and step into the road so a car has to swerve to pass. There's a screech of tyres and the sudden blaring of music … "America, okay by me in America …"

I understand,' I start to say, just as a car door bangs shut behind the line of Swishers.

'Sasha Baker,' announces the driver. 'Are you okay? I nearly hit you.'

100

Oh, not now, please not now, not now. The Swishers glare at me before turning to smile at Cass.

'You've got your own car?' says Chloe, purring like a cat. She slides a fingernail – the same one that was just wedged beneath my eyeball – down Cass's arm. He watches it as if it's an insect. 'Well, doesn't that just make you even more interesting, Cass Ely.'

He stares at her. 'It doesn't? Or it does? I don't understand. Anyway, I'm just checking on Sasha as her pulse rate is escalating.'

Chloe glares at me then sidles around Cass. 'I think all our pulses are escalating,' she mews again. Even for Chloe, Queen of Swishers, it's embarrassingly obvious.

Cass looks her up and down. 'No. Yours is surprisingly slow. You might have low blood pressure,' he announces.

I'm actually just wishing he'd run me over. This is painful from all directions. He couldn't be less bothered about Chloe, and this seems to just spark her into more and more pathetic flirting.

'Oh!' she says, sweeping her hair over her ear so that he can view her long, beautiful neck from the perfect angle. 'Are you a doctor too?'

Even Dana winces. 'Come on, Chloe. We'll be late for our lift.'

'Maybe Cass can give us a lift,' says Chloe, just as Cass frowns at her and asks, 'Too? As well as what? I'm not exactly a doctor, but as well as what? I don't understand.'

'As well as gorgeous,' purrs Chloe. India looks sick, and it seems for a moment as if even the Swishers' loyalty to their queen is wavering.

Which I can't allow to happen. If there's even a hint that Chloe's Pink Ladies have strayed from the path of Chloe-adoration and that it's because of Cass Ely who seems to only be bothered about me, then my life will become even more hell as she targets me over and over.

'Cass!' I bellow suddenly.

'Sasha Baker.'

'Could you give Chloe and the Sw … the others a lift? They'll all fit in your car.'

'What about you?' he asks.

Chloe sneers. 'Oh, she won't fit in your car.'

'Not with all of us in it,' adds Suzette hastily. She and India, at least, seem to have grasped that snubbing me in front of Cass Ely will not make him love Chloe. It might actually make him not like Chloe at all.

'What I meant,' says Chloe.

Cass peers down his regal nose at them all and then nods towards me. 'What do you think, Sasha?'

'It was my idea.'

'So it was.' He smiles brightly, his teeth even whiter than Annette's bleached babies. 'Then fine. Ladies, if you'd like to get in the car. Sasha?'

'I'm happy to walk. Need the fresh air. And don't want to be too early for work.'

'If you're sure?'

'So sure.'

And finally – finally! – he stops talking to me and follows the Swishers to his car which is some kind of open-topped sports number which must have cost him (or his parents) a bomb. I draw level with it as he folds his long body into the driver's seat. He's singing, and India is joining in with more energy than talent. 'I know a boat you can go on. Everyone there will give big cheer …'

They drive off, Cass waving a long, languid arm, as I gather myself together. He was right. My pulse rate is escalating, and it's not all because I'm upset. That strange feeling, the one from my dream the other night, has washed over me again.

He's saved me once more. Driving Chloe and the others away has nothing to do with him wanting to be with them, but everything to do with him getting them away from me. He's rescued me. Me, Sasha Baker.

And even my name feels special when he says it, which he does all the time, often, over and over, in full.

Cherished. I feel cherished.

I half-skip to Work Experience, feeling lighter than air. It's only when I reach the door of The Body Beautiful that it occurs to me why the music in his car was familiar, and why India sang along too.

The song is from West Side Story.

I push the door open, my heart beating faster than ever. Faster than is even possible.

Chapter 10 Another Work Experience Day

Breathe into the bag, Sasha. Come on. Good and deep.'

Annette forces it over my nose. My eyes may be a bit blurry, but the bag looks suspiciously like one of those paper jobs for disposing of sanitary towels. I splutter and try to bat it away.

'It's a new one, Sash,' says Annette, scrunching it back against my face. 'Now breathe. In. Out. In. Out.'

I do as I'm told, and suddenly feel my heart-rate slowing. I hadn't even been aware how badly it was racing – but now I recall that it felt like it was exploding through my chest before Annette made me remember to slurp air in and out of my lungs. My vision clears a bit as I peer at Annette over the crimped white edges of the paper bag.

'Why am I doing this?' I ask into it. The bag inflates rapidly then collapses into my mouth. 'Eugh.'

Annette removes it. 'You seemed to be having a panic attack. Stumbled through the door muttering something about Tony and feeling like … cherries? … before you keeled over on the Reception desk.'

Charlotte is perched on her Receptionist's bar stool, chewing her plump lower lip. 'I thought I'd done something terrible to you. Knocked you out with nail polish fumes or something. Are you okay?'

I don't know, am I? I want to ask. But I don't want to worry them any more than I already have. And anyway, how would they be able to answer? Am I? Because in a dream I got into a play with Cass Ely who didn't exist two days ago but now seems to be popping up all over my past at SkyDivers and school auditions, and very much in my present whenever the Swishers are around which incites them to hate me. Now, like Maria, they have HATE. I so preferred it when they didn't know I existed but now I am top of their hate hit list and basically doomed. As if I didn't already have enough doom going on, I also seem to have a stalker-stroke-wizard determined to make my life hell. Does that sound okay to you?

Freak out if I came out with all that? Massive. Annette would have to put a pillow case over my head to deal with all that.

So instead I just nod. 'Fine. I'm fine. Sorry I scared you.'

'Don't worry about that, it's all good,' says Charlotte, smiling but with a forehead furrowed like a Shar Pei puppy, so I know it's not all good at all. I've seen a lot of those smiles in my life. 'It's just that your friend is coming in today for a treatment, and I wanted you to—'

'Friend?' I yell. 'Which friend? I don't have any friends! If it's Cass Ely haunting me again, I will definitely faint.'

Annette and Charlotte both stare at my outburst, which even I know is over the top.

'Sorry,' I say again.

'You don't need to apologise.' Charlotte's doing her Shar Pei impression again. 'And anyway, it's not—'

'Not true,' interrupts Annette. She grabs hold of my hands. 'You do have friends. We're your friends now, and we are going to give you the best work experience week ever. You are going to have free make-overs every day, and we'll share the cleaning afterwards.'

Charlotte grins, properly this time. 'Yeah. It's not like we'll have any customers. You can be our model for the week!'

My eyes are filling up with moist evidence of gratitude. I'm not used to people being this nice. 'You shouldn't be giving me free treatments if you don't have any customers,' I squeak.

'Okay, you can just do the cleaning,' says Annette.

'No! No! I want the treatments!' I squeal, louder this time.

'Thought so.' Annette flashes her bleached teeth at me. 'How about a head massage to start? Release any tension headaches.'

'Yes! Then I can practice my micro-needling,' adds Charlotte, which frankly I'm less pleased about. But willing. Still willing to be surrounded by so much niceness.

'Grab your needles, Char!' cries Annette with huge gusto, like a pirate queen rallying her crew.

Charlotte giggles but shakes her head. 'I can't! Customer, remember?'

The customer is at the door, which tinkles melodically as he enters. 'Oh! He IS a friend,' I say.

The customer stares at us all staring at him. 'Have I missed something? Was I meant to pre-wax?' Felix rubs his eyebrows so they stand on end. I've seen smaller kittens. 'Are they just too much to handle?'

'Not if you're a sheep shearer,' I say seriously, but he's looking at Charlotte.

'No, absolutely not, yes, not a problem.' She's so undecided as to whether to nod or shake her head that she's making plus signs in the air with her nose. 'Errm – come this way.'

'Are you okay to do them, Char? I can squeeze Felix into my schedule.' Annette smiles brightly, but I can see that she's thinking that Charlotte may be in way over her head.

'I'm happy if you're happy … Char,' says Felix.

What is going on with him? As Charlotte gives him the puppy smile and opens the door for Felix, my heart suddenly goes out to him. He's trying to impress her, when actually she likes Cass. He's going through with a painful procedure – okay, I'm not sure it's painful but surely it will be agonising for Felix to have two large rectangular objects ripped off his face – and all for nothing. And then, worst of all, he will look like … like a Not-Felix without his eyebrows. The Swishers who are paying us far too much attention right now will bay for his blood. He'll be eyebrow-shamed all over Instagram in less time than it will take Charlotte to wax the beasties off.

And there's one more thing which I've only just realised. I love Felix' eyebrows! They're totally him, and make him unique, and even give him his own special language. What will his face look like without them? Just weird! And unFelixy! It will be the worst make-over ever! It will be a make-under!

He wiggles them at me one last time as he leaves Reception in Charlotte's jet-stream of perfume and tanning lotion. 'Say bye to the brows,' he mutters darkly, as if they're going to be shot off his face by a mafia drug lord.

I have to say something. 'You're making a mistake,' I whisper.

But the door has closed already. Annette wrinkles her own perfect eyebrows at me.

'Why's he making a mistake?'

'It's … it's not just one. It's several,' I say helplessly. 'I just don't want him to get hurt.'

'Oh.' She strokes my hair. 'Honestly, it's not that painful.'

I really don't want to go into it all with Annette, who was probably never bullied or held up for public ridicule. Mostly I don't want him to get his feelings torn up by chasing Charlotte, when she's into Cass. Cass Ely, eagle-eyed and ever present, even in my dreams and memories.

And suddenly I realise something. Cass is always around when I need saving, and in my do-overs. He has something to do with the do-overs. I might not have used them to good effect so far, but here is one I can really focus on.

In fact, if I can create another do-over moment, I can head Felix off at the door or something so he hangs onto his eyebrows and his inner Felixicity and avoid lasting outcast status at school.

'Annette!' I shout suddenly. 'What room are they in?'

She frowns. 'Left, I think.'

'Great! Can I … could you do my head massage in the right-hand room? Only I'm feeling a bit tense.'

'Oh, love.' She cups my face in her hands. 'You really are a worry-wort, aren't you? And you really shouldn't be – at your age you've got nothing to fear. Grab the future with both hands.'

As she takes hold of my future-grabbing hands, she glances at my dry-skinned fingers with their chewed-off nails and 'Buy cheese!' written on my left palm, and something sharpens in her eyes. She's figured something out. 'And in the meantime,' she continues smoothly, 'let's just get you that head massage. Then I'll leave you to … meditate.'

Sleep, is what she doesn't say but really means, because after she's unknotted all the nastiness out of my scalp and neck, she wraps me up in four blankets, puts a full proper pillow under my head and turns on the tinkly music. 'I'll just go and supervise next door,' she whispers. 'You close your eyes and think positive thoughts.'

I grin. 'That's exactly what I'll do.'

'Good.'

She's gone in a heartbeat, and I focus on positive thoughts.

'I'm positive I'm having do-overs. I'm positive Cass Ely is something to do with it. I'm positive I can use the do-overs properly if I can focus better. I'm positive – positive – that I'd like to do this morning all over again. I'm positive I can change it from before I went into school. Positive.'

Positive, positive, positive. I just repeat the word in my head — until the bed expands into a marshmallow and swallows me up in a deep, deep sleep.

Chapter 11 One year before

Breathe that in, Sash. What's that smell?' Someone beside me snorts in a vast throatful of oxygen as though the earth's about to run out of air. 'It's like honey!' she bellows. 'I love it here already! Air that smells like honey! Wow!'

The do-over plan has worked – but only sort of. I'm in school, for sure ... but not mine. And not earlier the same morning so that I can save Felix's eyebrows. I glance to my side and find Olivia scuffing along a corridor in her cleanest jeans and an inoffensive navy sweatshirt. She grins goofily at me and I notice how sweet she looks. She's younger and in non-trendy clothes and walking with a vague, happy skip every third or fourth step, which is something I know has been knocked out of her by the joint sneers of Tess and Danni, the pre-Swishers.

So this must be before Tess and Danni. Before private school. Olivia's Year 6, in fact.

Suddenly, Olivia grabs my arm. 'Is that him?' she hisses in such a stage whisper that the man she's talking about smothers a smile.

He's further along the corridor, which I see now is lined up to waist-height with beautiful wood panelling which accounts for the honey smell. As someone who knows their cleaning products, I recognise the scent of beeswax. Above the panels are photos of people in graduation gowns or accepting awards in scientific gatherings, all wearing cheesy grins.

'That's right. Former students,' I mutter as it comes back to me properly.

'Oh! I thought he was the principal!' sniggers Olivia, about to chummily high-five him or something.

'I … am the principal, but don't worry. Many people find it hard to believe,' says the man, at the same time as I whisper, 'Not him, the people in the photos!'

By now we've arrived at his door, so I gather my senses quickly and stick out my hand. 'Hello, Mr Warburton. I'm Sasha, Olivia's sister.'

He's polite enough not to look too confused. 'Sasha. Pleased to meet you. Is your mother meeting us here?'

'Nah. Mum has MS,' says Olivia cheerfully. 'She's having a bad day.'

Mr Warburton looks down at her with wonderfully kind brown eyes. 'Poor Mum,' he says with a nod. 'So it's all thanks to your sister for bringing you in for your interview, then, Olivia!'

'Yeah. She met me at my school gates.'

Olivia smiles at him but obviously isn't taking in the undercurrent, which is that Mr Warburton, like Annette, has figured a lot of stuff out in a few tiny moments. It's then that I remember, with something like a stabbing pain under my ribs, just why we wanted so much for Olivia to come to this school, with this gentle, wise man at the helm and its slightly crumbly walls layered with the aroma of beeswax and non-showy high achievement.

This day – this do-over - is her scholarship assessment. It's where we find out if she gets in – and of course I know that she does, because we've already lived it. In fact, this one's so in the bag that I wonder what I'm doing in this particular re-run. As it's already guaranteed, I relax a million times more than when I first actually walked Olivia from her primary school to the subtly-hidden private high school quite near our home.

The principal welcomes us into his room with a smile that is more familiar to me than to Olivia, because I've seen it dozens of times in the year that Liv's been at the school. He parks us both on the sofa and sits at the Liv end of it on a small wooden chair. 'So, Olivia Baker, you've made a very good impression at your current school. Top of the class, I hear?'

She wrinkles her nose. 'Only sometimes.'

'Would you like it to be all the time?' he asks.

Olivia thinks about it, then shrugs. 'I don't mind, really. It totally matters to some people, doesn't it? I mean,' she adds, sitting forward as she remembers something specific, 'Jayden Smith's dad said he'd buy him a PlayStation if he beat me in the end-of-year tests, so he tried extra hard and he beat me!'

'And got a PlayStation?' says the Principal, all sorts of other questions playing across his face.

'He did! But he really wanted one, so I didn't mind coming second.' She grins cheerfully, with the complete sweetness she always had before Tess and Danni.

'So you're a team player.' Mr Warburton nods with approval. 'And you like team sports, too. Soccer, is it?'

'Yes!' Olivia lays a hand across her chest, her eyes dramatically round. 'I love football even more than Jayden loves his PlayStation!'

The Principal grins. 'Can you help us win the local league?'

'I'll do my best,' she says seriously.

He lifts his hand and they fist-bump, and I suddenly wonder if this is the moment she gets in. In the now, the First Eleven are powering through a great season, and Liv has been a major player – mostly by rolling in mud, if the laundry is anything to go by.

As if he's reading my mind, Mr Warburton says, 'Of course, it creates a huge amount of washing.' He glances at me.

'We'll manage,' I tell him, and I know he knows that I really mean that *I* will manage, because I do. But then I remember something I've been saying to myself all year, and decide it's worth a shot. 'Although a second set of kit would be helpful. If Liv gets in!' I laugh as if we don't expect it to happen.

Mr Warburton notes something down on his pad, then points his pen at me. 'That, Sasha, is a very good idea. And the same for uniform, I suppose?'

Wow and hell yes. 'That would be great! If she gets in.'

'Good,' he announces, as if it's settled. 'And what about you, Sasha?' he says with a sudden change of tack. 'Maybe we should have both sisters here. You're Year 11, yes?'

'Yes, but … no,' I say automatically, exactly as I said last time. 'The sixth form is fee-paying, isn't it?'

'So is the school, as you know, but there are ways for deserving students to get support.'

He'd said that last time, and I sigh a little. 'It will just be great if Liv gets to come here.' One less thing for me to worry about, I think but don't say, but it's almost as if there's a speech bubble coming out of my brain – a speech bubble that Mr Warburton reads in a flash.

He nods, clearly deciding not to press the matter. Then he smiles at Olivia. 'Well, I think I can put you both out of your misery. Olivia, I'm delighted to confirm that you're invited to Fieldings school on a full scholarship, if you'd like to join us here.'

Olivia goggles at me and then leaps up from the sofa. 'Yes! I would like to join you here!'

'Excellent.'

She squeaks and jumps around a bit. 'Can I hug you?'

'Um, no,' says the head, 'but we can double high-five, if you like.'

'High-ten!' she bellows with both hands in the air.

As Mr Warburton smacks her palms with a grin, he murmurs from the corner of his mouth, 'Oh, what have we done?' to me, and I know that he completely, completely gets her and she will do wonderfully well here.

'I don't think you can back out now, sir,' I say gently.

'Wouldn't dream of it,' he replies. 'Now, Olivia, if you'd like to take this note along to the uniform shop by the front office and ask for two football kits and two full sets of school uniform, we'll get you sorted while you're here. Might as well make everything as easy as possible. You'll get a laptop on your first day, fully funded, and if you ever need anything during what I'm sure will be a very successful time at Fieldings, you or Sasha or your mum can just let me know. Okay?'

'Okay!' she hollers with joy.

Mr Warburton hands her his scribbled note for the uniform shop and walks us to the door. I'm just about to leave when I think of something. There must be some reason we're doing this again, after all. 'Mr Warburton,' I say hesitantly, 'when Olivia starts here, could you try to make sure ...'

He prompts me when I don't finish. 'Anything I can do.'

'I think Olivia needs friends who are kind of like her. A bit clever, into sports, but all sort of low-key. We have a lot going on at home and it would help if she didn't get

116

too much peer pressure about stuff she doesn't have and can't do and so on.'

'PlayStations?'

'More like weekend clothes and horses.'

'Got it. No Mean Girls. I'll mention it to the Head of Year.'

'Thank you.' I pump his hand up and down in the way my dad would have done, because sometimes I have to be Mum and sometimes Dad. 'That would be amazing.'

What a brilliant principal. I compare him with Mrs Stewart and it's like one of them is an actual person and one is an alien. She'd probably have gone out of her way to make sure Liv was paired up with future Swishers, and I feel a sudden intense relief that Liv's life will be just a tiny bit easier when she starts at this gorgeous school.

A gorgeous school that I could be at too, if I was a deserving student who could get support. I steer Liv towards the uniform shop which I'd spotted as we came in, and as she springs down the corridor like a tween-sized, excited flea, we pass little studio rooms from which music floats accompanied by laughter and strangled attempts at singing, followed by more laughter. One of the doors swings open and a couple of boys and a girl about my age stagger through the door, carrying a full-sized papier mache gladiator.

'Sorry!' cries the girl as the statue's spear pokes me in the shoulder. 'Gluteus Maximus just won't behave himself!'

'His name's Mark Anthony!' groans the nearest boy.

'I meant you,' she tells him with a grin.

They head off towards the hall where some kind of performance is going on – or rather, being rehearsed. That's right. I can picture it now. In the first term of Olivia's first year at Fielding's, the sixth-form drama group stages 'Anthony and Cleopatra', broken down for the audience into understandable chunks with a cartoon version running on a big screen to one side.

Lordy times a million how I want to come to this school. How much I want to come here for my last couple of years before college (that's college for other people, because I'll need to be at home with Mum) and all of that teen stuff I'm meant to be enjoying.

I stop so abruptly at the uniform shop counter that Olivia bashes into my back.

'Sash-aaaaaa!'

The lady from the office who has quickly taken over shop duties raises her eyebrows in amusement. I decide to trust her and hand her the note from the principal. 'Mr Warburton says Liv should have two sets of everything including soccer strip,' I say quickly. 'Would you be able to kit her out?'

She smiles at Olivia. 'You got in, then! Superb. Right, well, let's try on this jumper and start from there.'

'Yessss!' Olivia hauls the new sweater over her head as I step away from the door. 'Where are you going, Sash?'

'Just … something I have to do.' I'm missing a chance, I can feel it. I'm not going to miss it again, for Felix or anyone – eyebrows or no eyebrows. 'I'll be back in a second.'

Heart pounding and back no doubt jiggling as I rush along the corridor to stop my courage from running out, I race back to the Principal's office and tap on the door.

Mr Warburton opens it himself. 'Did she forget something?' he says in the manner of someone who already knows Olivia better than she knows herself.

'No, I did. I … I mean …' I gulp in a great shaky breath and somehow it steadies me. 'What would I have to do to get a scholarship to the sixth form?'

'Well, we'd need to see your results, of course,' he says with a bored shrug, as if he couldn't care less about results. 'But I'm assuming they're fine. Mainly what the Trustees need to see is an essay about your life, and why and how you think Fieldings would …' He pauses thoughtfully. '… help.'

Why and how Fieldings would help? Help with my terrible vie? Has he got that wrong? 'Don't you mean how I'd help Fieldings? Be a proud ambassador and all that?'

Perching on the arm of the sofa, Mr Warburton fixes his kind Labrador eyes on my scarlet face. 'We like to support our students here, Sasha. I'd like you to think about what kind of support you'd need to do whatever you want to do and be in life, and tell us about it in an essay. Just three pages.'

'Is … is that all?'

He smiles. 'You can start now, if you like,' he says, and before I have chance to argue he steers me by the elbow to one of the little studies across the hall and sits me down at a computer. He even opens a Word document for me. 'I'll leave you to it. Three pages. Pour it onto the page! Then email it to Mrs Powell in the office. The email address is on the wall there.'

For a moment, after he's left, I sit chewing my thumbnail, wondering if I dare do this. I can't. I don't dare. But then ... this is it, my do-over. I know it. A do-over where India won't get the part because I let her, and Work Experience day will be making gladiators for a theatre company. Where Liv and I walk up to school together and I'll be able to leave later and spend more time with Mum. Where Mum can worry less and maybe even get better.

I know that's not going to happen, though, and in the end that's where I start, picking out the letters one by one at first, as I choose my words carefully, but then flowing faster and faster as the raw, ugly and yet sometimes beautiful details of my life tumble across the screen.

My mum has MS. It's non-curable, unless science comes up with a miracle remedy in the next few years. My dad died a few years ago in ... well, a terrible night that I don't like to think about too much. I've been taking care of my sister, Olivia, since that night, while trying to make it seem like Mum actually does it all so she can hang onto some shred of self-respect, as she puts it. I have to tell you, I have nothing but respect for my mum. She's awesome.

This morning, a friend told me I might be susceptible to MS too. There's a genetic marker of some kind which

120

means it might be hereditary. They've never told us this at the hospital so it was kind of a shock – another shock in my slightly shocking life. I got cross with my friend, even though it's not his fault. He's only trying to help, as he always is.

I'd tell you about a typical day in my life, and why Fieldings would help with that, but I don't have many typical days. Sometimes Mum can't get down the stairs, so I have to call George – that's our support worker – to come to the house early. Sometimes there's stuff to sign and do for Olivia that's hard to do because I'm not her guardian, I'm just her sister – but if Mum can't hold the pen that day ... well, I have to figure something out. I do laundry. A lot of laundry. And I can never tell for sure what time I'm going to be somewhere, which gets me into a heap of trouble at school where nobody really gets it. Don't get that I'm really a kid, doing the job of a nurse and a helper and a cleaner and a sister and a mother. And sometimes a father.

Actually that's not true. Felix gets it, and his mum looks out for me, too. I've just met Annette and Charlotte at my work experience at The Body Beautiful, and I think they get it too. But mostly I'm either invisible, or visible for the wrong reasons.

As to how Fieldings would help with that? I don't honestly know. But I can feel the kindness here, so strong it makes me gasp like someone squashed in a beautiful bear hug. I think one of the ways I could be visible for the right reasons would be singing, or theatre – or both. I don't get the opportunity at my current school for that, and I suspect it will only get tougher in Year 12 ...

On I ramble, purging verbally, saying things I haven't really told anyone but Felix and George and the people who are already aware anyway – apart from I don't moan about it to Mum and Liv.

Suddenly I'm on the top of the third page.

'*So not having to get the bus would make life so much easier, because it's not just the timing of the bus which is awkward, but the forms I have to get Mum to sign on a good day and then send in to get the bus pass, and the money we have to find if I don't manage to do that in time, and the catch-up on all the things I'm late for because I miss the bus or can't afford it that day – which I never tell Mum. She worries enough ...*'

I stop abruptly as Liv slams through the door bearing armfuls of uniform and kit. 'What happened to you? You said you'd be a second!' The clothes are muffling her voice, but she sounds more excited than annoyed. 'Look at all this STUFF!' she shrieks, and then she dumps it all on my keyboard.

For a moment, I think she's destroyed my letter, but then I see her name blinking at me from behind a pale green shirt collar, and it's still there. I save it quickly, trying not to re-read it at the same time ... but there it is. All that self-pitying rubbish. How is that going to get me a scholarship? Wasn't I meant to talk about my achievements and awards and what I'm going to give back to humanity through scientific research? The only science

I've mentioned is the genetic disaster of my life. What have I been thinking?

I scoop up bottle-green uniform in my left arm and grab Olivia with the right. 'Come on, we've been ages. Mum will be wondering where we are.'

Liv squeals. 'Wait till I tell her I'm in! And we've already got the stuff!'

To my shame and self-loathing disgust, I have to blink back a tear. She's in … and I'm not. Not with the moany old bilge I've just stuck on the computer.

Summoned by the siren of Liv, Mr Warburton pops his head out of his door. 'See you soon, Olivia! And you too, Sasha! Did you send it to Mrs Powell?'

'Yes!' I say brightly. 'Just now!' His smile falters at my brittle fakeness, but I plough on anyway. 'Thanks so much, Mr Warburton! Olivia will see you next term!' I've become so shrill that I'm nearly as loud as Liv.

'Look forward to it,' he says after the tiniest, most microscopic pause. 'Genuinely.'

'Bye, Mr Warbleford!' cries Olivia.

'It's not … come on, Liv. Time to go,' I say quickly. Any more of his shrewd nods and pauses and I'll confess: 'No, I didn't send the essay! I didn't even finish it! So no, I won't be coming here, because I'm too miserable for this happy, lively place!'

I run for the door before I crumble, nudging my sister ahead of me, ignoring the feeling of Labrador eyes boring into the back of my skull and the gales of laughter from the drama studio. 'Stop that. You're a pain in the gladiator, Lucas!'

I would like it here so much and have screwed it up so spectacularly that my heart begins to hurt. Planting a hand on Liv's shoulder for secret support as my vision swims, I close my eyes against the pain. I missed the real chance of a do-over. I keep missing the do-over opportunities. So what, exactly, is the point of it all?

Chapter 12 WE Day again

Breathe on her own. I can promise you she doesn't need a ventilator,' rants a cross male voice.

'Are you sure?' That's Felix. 'Or are you just saying that because there aren't any available?'

The doctor – I can see him now through a tiny slit between my eyelids, youngish and tired and a little irritated – sighs loudly. 'No. I am saying that because she doesn't need one. She had a panic attack. Very common.' His tone softens when he looks around Felix to the other person in the room. 'You did the right thing bringing her in, both of you, but your friend is going to be fine.'

'But she's a suspect for Multiple Sclerosis!' cries Felix.

'Susceptible,' I mutter hoarsely, as my brain starts to spin. Don't want to be here. Hate being here. Why am I here? 'He means I'm susceptible.'

The doctor spins towards me. 'Ah. Awake. Well, trust me, MS is not what you've got now.'

'Can you check, though, Doctor?' blurts an anxious voice. A beautiful golden face hovers above me. 'She couldn't even remember who I was when I woke her up. Kept saying I was a painful radiator. I had to say, Sasha, it's me, babes! Charlotte!'

Why was I calling her a radiator? Then I remember. 'Was it … gladiator?'

'See? Why would you be calling Charlotte a gladiator?' Felix drops down beside the bed so his face lines up with mine. His eyebrows are still huge, thankfully. Maybe the do-over did work! 'Doctor, she's losing it! Are you sure she's not horribly sick?'

The doctor metes out another long-suffering sigh. 'I'll have her bloods re-done,' he says to placate them, although it sounds very similar to the way I've just told Mr Warburton that

yes, I sent the essay. Not that I just did that, of course. That was over a year ago. 'And we'll send them to Miss Baker at home. Is someone coming for her …' he asks bluntly, as if he just left off the word "body" and I'm actually dead.

I want to scream but I don't have enough energy to force my voice up through my throat. Nooooo! Nobody is coming for me, because I'm it! I'm the somebody who goes for people, since the terrible night in my terrible life – the last time I was in here, actually, which is why I'm in a panic.

Ah. A do-over? Am I now getting back-to-back do-overs?

Even if I am, how could I ever do that horrible, awful night again, when Dad decided enough was enough …

'She should stay in for observation,' says Charlotte, suddenly sounding very official and grown-up until I notice she's checking her phone. Annette must be feeding her lines from the salon. 'She might have concussion.'

'Did she fall over?'

'No, she passed out on a bed.'

'So how do you know she wasn't just asleep?'

Charlotte glances at her phone. 'Her pulse rate appeared to have dropped and she was unresp ... unresponsive.'

'Until she started shouting about gladiators?' says the man with a tiny snarl.

Felix's eyebrows drift out of view as he straightens up. 'Well, that's very out of character. That might be a sign of brain damage.'

No longer mesmerised by her golden prettiness, the doctor glares from Charlotte to Felix and towards the door, then grabs the little clipboard from the end of my bed. 'Okay. Bloods. Observation overnight if we don't need the bed for a genuine emergency,' he snaps. 'And then home in the morning, with an actual adult. Is someone calling her mother?'

'Uh-hum, my mother, yes,' says Felix vaguely.

'You're ... you're her brother?'

Eyebrows contorting as he tries to think how to answer that, Felix opens his mouth to speak but Charlotte suddenly pipes up. 'Oh, there's her brother! Look, he's an actual adult. Leave it with us, Doctor, and we'll be out of your hair in no time.'

'I don't have a brother,' I tell Felix, my tongue so thick it feels like a rug.

'See? Delusional,' says Felix.

I close my eyes again, nauseous with confusion. Awake or in a do-over? Sick or not sick? With my usual family set up of Mum and Liv or in a new one where Felix is my brother, which I really, really hope isn't the case? .

'Maybe it is a good idea if I stay the night, Charlotte,' I whisper. 'I'm very confused.'

She gazes at me from under her fake lashes. 'Oh, poor Sasha. You've really been through it! Look, the doctor's gone and Felix ran off to talk to your family,' she says, adding air quotes around the word "family". 'So let's make you all comfortable and I'll tell you what happened.' She mummifies my feet in a scratchy blanket, props my head on a couple of pillows and inserts a cushion off the visitor's chair under my knees. 'Sorry, I only know how to do it beautician style.'

'It's great.' It truly is very comfortable. If it wasn't all so weird, I'd have another nap. But I really don't like it here. 'I have to get home though …'

'Felix will sort it.' She seems to be very close to Felix all of a sudden. 'Don't you worry about anything, okay? I'll explain it all.' Charlotte settles onto the bed to tell me her yarn. 'Anyway, what happened was that Felix suddenly decided he didn't want his eyebrows waxed so I came in to tell you he was leaving, in case you wanted to say goodbye, and you were lying flat on your back like one of those bodies on a tomb as if you were dead asleep, but your eyes were open! And they were all white like a zombie's but brighter and shinier, and I honestly thought you'd died but then you sat up and shouted the painful radiator thing and Felix told me and Auntie A what happened this morning with the genetic suspects and we all agreed you should go to hospital.'

'All? Where's Annette then?'

'At the shop. She was on the phone to a woman about a party. A party!'

Maybe the party woman is George. If it's George, that's an actual recent conversation and I'm definitely not in a do-over. 'I need to get home, Charlotte.'

'But the bloods!' Charlotte's eyes grow round. 'And the observations!'

'I feel fine, and I need to go – and you don't need to come with me,' I add before she offers. I just need to get out of this place and back to the house on my own, before Mum panics again. I definitely do not need her to know I've been in hospital. Particularly this hospital.

'All right, Lovely, if you're sure,' says Charlotte. ' I'll just make sure the doctor's got your deets for the results.' She grins from the doorway. 'I quite like this! Feels like Casualty.'

'It literally is Casualty.'

'No, the programme, silly! Maybe I'll retrain as a nurse,' she adds thoughtfully, waving as she goes off in search of McDreamy or whoever may next fall under her bronzed enchantment. Felix. Cass. The doctor. At least she's nice and deserves the attention, unlike some swishy people I know ...

Un-swaddling my ankles from the hospital blanket, I clamber unsteadily to my feet and look around for my things. My coat's been thrown onto the next bed, so I shuffle towards it, feeling better with each step although I'm aware that the do-overs seem to be taking more out of me each time they happen. In the doorway, I peer left down the corridor to locate Charlotte and the deets. Not there. I peer right instead - and have near heart failure all over again.

Felix is having a full-on argument with the person they are pretending is my brother. Again, and for some reason that I'm not sure I want to confront, I'm glad that this person is also not actually my brother. Cass Ely looms over Felix like a Hemsworth, hands on his hips, shaking his tawny head and trying to interrupt the stream of angry words pouring from Felix's mouth. I can't make them all out but am pretty sure I hear what the doctor was saying about bloods and observation, lots more about observation, and then he points his finger at Cass's slightly beaky nose and shouts, 'No! Stop interfering!'

Cass reels upward in shock at Fierce Felix, whose face is more thunderous than I've ever seen it. Is Cass interfering? I get the sense he's only trying to help. To help and cherish me. I could take a bit more interference like that, to be honest.

'She needs to stay here,' growls Felix.

'But I just thought …' says Cass, spreading his palms wide.

'You're not meant to think! Or do! You're just meant to observe!'

So he *had* brought Cass in to do overnight observations! Weird.

'What if she doesn't want to stay?' asks Cass reasonably. 'This place must bring back awful memories—'

'It does!' I call from the doorway. 'I want to go home!'

They both look round, a pair of naughty school-boys caught where they shouldn't be.

'He's … dabbling!' says Felix. 'Sticking his great big nose in where he shouldn't.'

'He's not. He's trying to do what I ask. You're the one who's interfering, Felix – making me stay when I don't want to; getting strangers to watch me overnight.'

'That's not what I meant!'

'So what did you mean then? I thought you were my friend! You're … you're my only friend, Felix! Why don't you know me better?'

Felix stares at me with the kind of stunned expression you see on people in movies who've just been shot. I can imagine him pawing at the blossoming red stain on his chest, staggering a little and blinking rapidly as the truth sinks in that he's about to die as he slides down the wall, smearing scarlet blood across the white paint ...

'I do,' he says helplessly. 'I do know you better.'

'You don't seem to.'

Cass keeps out of it, a smidge embarrassed but watching us both carefully.

'Sorry, Sash. Really.' Felix looks wounded. 'Look, I've called my mum, she'll be here as soon as the staff meeting's finished,' he explains.

It'll be too late. 'I can't wait until then. Mum will worry.'

Cass nods, as if he knows the first thing about my mum. Maybe he's observed her, too, through our back window. 'See? She needs to go home now. Come on, Sasha. I've got transport.'

Of course you have, wonderful Cass, I think dreamily. I picture myself in the red sports car … and shake my head. 'I can't go in your car. The Swish … India and Dana and the others will kill me if they see me.'

At the same moment, each of them cocks their head on one side, birdlike, and gazes at me – an eagle and a real-life Angry Bird, equally confused. 'Sasha, they…' starts Felix with a sigh.

'Okay. No car,' cries Cass. 'I have other transport. Come with me.'

Felix glares at him. 'Where? How?'

'I have ways,' said Cass mysteriously. 'You'll fit in too, if you like?'

'I'd better go with Charlotte,' mutters Felix. 'She's only just passed her test, and she gets nervous on her own.'

Not for the first time, I wonder just how long I was passed out at the salon or in this hospital. When did everyone to get so chummy and find out each other's life histories?

Unable to meet my eye as he trudges past, Felix heads toward the main doors in search of Charlotte. Cass just grins and spins off in the opposite direction. 'This way, Sasha Baker.'

Without a moment's hesitation, he lopes along the corridors, straight through several wards and in one side of a nurse's kitchen and out the other without breaking his stride. I scuttle along in his wake, hoping nobody stops us and asks exactly what we're doing in Neo-Natal or Oncology, or the diagnostics area where my doctor is studying someone's notes with another doctor, too busy to notice a tall teen and a shorter former patient in their midst.

Suddenly Cass bursts through some double doors and we find ourselves in a parking bay, somewhere around the side of the hospital. Striding to a nearby vehicle, he opens the passenger door for me and bows to let me enter the cab.

'Are you kidding me?'

'Genuinely not. I've found I'm not good at jokes.'

'No, I mean, you can't seriously expect me to get in there?'

Cass frowns, then his face clears. 'Ah! You want to get in the back?

'No, Cass. I don't want to get in it at all.'

It's an ambulance. Possibly not a nee-naw, race-through-the-city-with-lights-ablaze ambulance, but definitely a medical vehicle used for transporting sick people. People like my mum. And like my dad. I'm starting to hyperventilate again. Seriously, who is this guy?

'Are you trying to steal it?'

'No. People round here know me. I work here some of the time. It's allowed.'

'So why didn't you say so at Work Experience Day?' I squeak.

'Sasha Baker, I think you should get in the back with the medical equipment. Your pulse rate is too rapid again.'

'I don't want to!' I whisper frantically, but it sounds horribly childish, as if I'm about to follow up with, 'You can't make me!'

But it seems he can actually make me, because suddenly Cass Ely walks over and grabs hold of both my hands.

'I know you're scared, Sasha Baker. I know this makes you remember things you don't want to and feel things you don't wish to feel. But you will be fine. You'll be fine with me. Make the most of it.' He leans his face towards mine and I watch the flecks of gold swim around in his green eyes like magical Koi carp in a beautiful Japanese garden. 'Make the most of the moment.'

So I do. I climb into the passenger seat beside him and try not to think about ambulances and the people in them – apart from the two people in this very ambulance, in this very now-ish moment. Me. And hunched behind the steering wheel, the Swishers' idol, Cass Ely.

Chapter 13 Nowness

Breathe right down into your lungs. It helps keep you calm if you're stressed.'

Cass is in instruction mode as he steers the ambulance deftly across town. Surprisingly for a newcomer, he knows every back road and short cut almost instinctively. Maybe he's not such a newcomer, after all, though. He does work at the hospital already, after all. And he is in my do-overs from several months ago. Of course he's not that new. In fact, when I glance at him sideways, trying not to let him see me checking him out in case he thinks I'm checking him out, he suddenly looks really old, like the papier mache gladiator. I have a small panic in case he's actually forty years old and is kidnapping me for human trafficking. Who would look after everyone if that happened?

Cass looks directly at me while swinging the ambulance right around a blind corner. 'Really, Sasha Baker. Breathe.'

'It's your driving! Look at the road!'

'Nope. The extra panic started before then. Your heart rate is going through the roof again.'

'How can you tell?' I ask carefully, in case heart monitoring is a skill that forty-year-old human traffickers have developed.

For a split second he stares at the ambulance dials and speedometers, and then he smiles. 'You're in an advanced medical vehicle. The seat transmits information to the dashboard. It's right before my eyes.'

'Seriously? That's amazing. Can I see—'

'Here we are!' he choruses like a Glee star, yanking on the handbrake and leaning across me to open my door. His arm is sculpted like marble, and I try hard not to stare as he nods towards the door. 'Can you get out or do you need to be on a stretcher? Maybe a wheelchair?'

'No!' I snap, rather too loudly. 'There really can't be more than one of us in the house needing wheelchairs and stretchers.'

Cass watches my face dispassionately, then nods. 'True. Your mother has a debilitating disease which requires her to be in a wheelchair, and your father needed stretchers and emergency treatment and then died suddenly which is something you don't want to be reminded of, and you are in charge of the household, effectively, including looking after your younger sister. I get it. A second wheelchair would not be helpful.'

It's a bald statement of fact, of truth, and I absolutely know every aspect of it, of course – but hearing him say it out loud makes my eyes fill with tears. 'No, it wouldn't,' I whisper.

'Your heart is getting fluttery again.'

'You didn't look at the dials.'

He stares straight at me, his mind ticking away. 'True. Now I'm observing physical signs. Watery eyes, heightened colour.' He peers at me more closely and I'm pretty sure my heart flutters harder. 'Blotchy neck and sweaty forehead,' he finishes.

Okay! Done. I drop down from the cabin onto the verge in front of our house. Anyone else might have expected curious neighbours to rubber-neck or even a few calls of concern from passing dog-walkers at the sight of an ambulance, but this is my house. People are kind of used to it. George turns up every day in a mini-van that's been especially adapted for wheelchair access; she's promising to teach me how to drive it as soon as I get my learner's license and she sorts out the insurance. And let's face it, we have had the odd few nee-naw-and-flashing-lights moments over recent years. So no one, not a soul, bats an eyelid when I slam the passenger door shut and head up the ramp to the door, calling out 'I'm home! I'm here! Everything's fine!' as I rattle the key in the door.

There's nobody in the house. Nobody. It's so weird at this time of day that I think I must be overlooking something, like a full-grown woman or two and the world's loudest tween. I find myself running round the house, checking in cupboards and behind doors as if it's a game of hide and seek. 'Mum? Olivia?'

I check my watch to find it's just past three o'clock. George should be here at this time – or actually, not here, but picking up Liv from school for football practice. But where is Mum? My stomach twists. Maybe she was in the hospital in some nearby ward while I was lying being fussed over for a panic attack. Was that why I was there? To save Mum?

Then my phone trills. It's a text from Felix. *RU OK?*

Yes, but at home and nobody's here.

All at Fieldings, he replies.

All? Who's all? And how does Felix know?

I rush back down the path and jump in the ambulance before Cass can drive off. 'Can you take me to Liv's school? It's—'

'I know it,' says Cass, and the vehicle is in gear and careering off towards Fieldings in a split second. It's close enough to walk, of course, but I have a growing sense of doom and want to get there quickly … and without running off down the street with visible back-jiggle, seeing as Cass is so good at pointing out tiny physical details.

We careen through the opening in the tall hedge so soon that it's as if the ambulance got there in one leap. 'Better slow down,' I tell Cass. 'We don't want anyone to think it's an emergency.'

'I don't believe anyone thinks that.'

He gestures through the windscreen to the gaggle of people standing on the sweep of gravel at the main door – or sitting, in my mum's case. They're all laughing and chatting without a care in the world. George is in deep conversation with Charlotte, who looks impossibly glamorous against a crumbly school backdrop. Liv and Felix are kicking the football to each other while Mum, squinting up into the sunshine, says something to Mr Warburton and Felix's mother that makes them both laugh and glance towards the flying soccer ball. Mum catches sight of us and raises her hand. A good day. She's having a really good day.

So that's the 'All' who's at Fieldings. My entire family and George who's basically family anyway, Charlotte, Felix and his mum and the Fieldings principal, having a jolly get-together of a garden party. For some reason, the general sense of ease and fun makes me furious.

I stomp across the gravel, wondering why Felix is here and his mother and his Charlotte. I mean, Charlotte. She's clearly not his because she spots Cass behind me and makes a bee-line for him, practically glowing with excitement and subtle glittery make-up. 'Feeling okay?' she calls as our paths cross. I nod, because I'm physically okay, though some kind of animal appears to be gnawing through my guts.

'Mum! What's going on? Why are you here?'

She smiles and frowns at the same time. 'I am allowed out, you know.'

'Yes. Sorry. I just mean … how?'

Felix's mother speaks up instead. 'It's my doing! Felix and Charlotte mentioned you might be a bit late back from work and Liv might need a lift, so I dashed round to find out if I could help and we got talking – it's been ages, hasn't it, Freya?'

'Too long, Lorraine! And so I said to George, "it's about time I saw this school and met the principal I hear so much about" and George offered to bring me down here. It's been lovely!' says Mum. 'Really uplifting.'

I can see that it has. She looks better than she has in ages, with a fresh pink tinge to her cheeks and clear eyes, free – for now – from pain.

'You never said your mum was an artist, Olivia,' says Mr Warburton to my sister. She stares at my mother in amazement.

'Oh, I haven't really done any in years, what with …' She flops her hand around in her lap. 'Olivia's never actually seen me in artist mode. I don't suppose even you remember it, do you, Sasha?'

I want to cry. Of course I do. I remember tea being late when someone other than me used to make it, because a painting needed to be finished. I remember Dad viewing the latest portrait, shaking his head in admiration. I remember it all, but it's pre-history. Pre the terrible night history. I can't tell her all that, so I just take hold of her good hand. 'I do remember.'

'You should give it another go,' says Mr Warburton. 'We could use some expertise with the theatres sets and so on.'

'Oh, I couldn't,' she says automatically, but we can all see the idea penetrating her brain. Maybe she could.

The principal smiles. 'Think about it?'

'I … will.'

This is all so surreal I can barely take it in. It's got the slight shimmery quality of a do-over. Maybe they're starting to merge with real life so I can't tell the difference between do-over and do-now, with Mum looking bright and happy, Felix and his mother chatting to George about eyebrows and facial treatments as if they're all wanna-be Swishers, Mr Warburton mentally giving Olivia house points for having an artistic mother, and somewhere behind me, Cass and Charlotte standing casually among us trying to pretend they're not totally gorgeous, like A-list film-stars shopping in an everyday supermarket. It's all completely freaky.

Felix suddenly glances behind me, and I feel a little sorry for him. No matter how nice and funny he is, Felix can't compete with Cass. He catches my eye and walks to my side.

'Thanks for covering for me,' I say.

He looks suddenly relieved. 'I thought you might be cross. Interfering again.'

'It is a bit interfery,' I say. 'But I understand why this time. I don't understand all the stuff in the hospital, though. Asking Cass to get involved?'

His eyebrows knit together as he considers how to respond. 'I agree,' he says finally. 'You have no idea how much that's backfired. Total mistake.'

Right. Charlotte. Currently being swept out from under Felix's eyebrows. Um, nose. I nudge him sympathetically, suddenly recalling that my friend was looking out for me, and that he has feelings.

'Does that mean I'm forgiven?' he whispers.

'Guess so. And just to thank you for being there for me, I'm going to do something for you. I'll distract Cass, and you grab Char's attention.'

'Char?' he repeats, not sure what or who I mean.

'Charlotte. Char is what Annette calls her. And you know what? I'm sure Cass is too obvious for her. She'll choose you in the end.'

'Me?'

'Yes, you.' I laugh suddenly. 'Hey, this is like normal teenager stuff! He likes her but she likes him and they like each other but don't dare mention it. I've never done this before!'

'Um, I bet you have,' he yelps uncomfortably, but I'm already marching across to the adults and my sister, delighted that I can introduce them to someone very cool and very interesting and, let's face it, hot, who actually seems to like me. Cherish me, even.

'Mum, George,' I announce, 'you should come and meet Cass Ely.'

'Is that the guy near the ambulance?' blurts Mr Warburton. 'He must be a former student, though I don't recognise the name. He looks awfully familiar.'

'Maybe. And he also works at the hospital. Anyway, he can tell you himself. Come on.'

But just as everyone smiles at me and George turns Mum's chair to help her over the grassy bumps, there's a screech of wheels and the ambulance takes off across the forecourt and out through the gap in the hedge.

Felix turns back towards us all with a shrug. 'Charlotte needed to get back to The Body Beautiful,' he calls, trying not to sound bitter. 'She says she'll see you tomorrow, Sash.'

'Oh,' I say, also trying not to sound bitter.

'Never mind,' says Felix's mum, though I'm not sure who she's saying it to. 'It's time I got back to work, too. I left in a rush!'

'Ah yes! The enemy school.' Mr Warburton grins. 'We always need people here, you know, if you fancy a change. Mrs Banner is close to retiring.'

'Did we just stumble into your recruitment drive?' asks Mum with a laugh.

'Not really. We just like good people around us,' he replies carefully. 'Talking of which, Sasha, when you have a moment, it would be great to have a chat.'

He sounds like he means a moment right now. But I don't. I don't have a moment. I have a world that is warping out of recognition, and an increasingly confusing whirlwind of new and scary emotions whipping about in my stomach, as if I didn't have enough scary emotions in there already.

'Thanks,' I say to the principal. 'I'll call in when I'm dropping Olivia off. Or picking her up. Or some time like that. Right now, we all need to get home.'

Everyone else looks perfectly happy not being at home, of course, so I'm aware this isn't true. I need to get home. I want some familiarity. Some routine. Something I recognise and understand, before I drop to the gravelly ground and Groundhog-Day my way through the last few hours, over and over again until I wake up a hundred years old or actually die.

But there's no sign of doing it over, so I pick up Liv's laptop bag and walk off down the drive, feeling more alone and confused in this lively gathering than ever before in my lonely and confusing life. At least at home I understand it. At least, at home, I know who I am.

Chapter 14 Groundhog WE Day

Breathe in like this, okay,' says Olivia from near my right shoulder, 'and your boobs get bigger!'

I stare at her, horrified. Mum's face as George pushes her along the street is a picture of terror, disbelief, amusement and a bit more terror. 'Who told you that?' she asks eventually, plumping for the only question that doesn't automatically lead to trouble.

I know who's told her that before she even answers. The pre-Swishers. 'Danni told me. Look, it works!' Cheeks turning purple from holding her breath, she rolls back her shoulders and struts along the pavement.

'Liv, stop it!' I glance around, hoping somehow that Felix and his mum won't have heard it as they drive past – but then this is Olivia we're talking about, so they're sharing expressions of sympathy and trying not to laugh as their car trundles by. 'Anyway, you don't have boobs!'

'I nearly do!' she cries.

Mum shakes her head, whispering, 'Good lord, it's started!'

'Anyway, Danni and Tess were just saying …' Teasing, I'm guessing. '… that it's time I started looking like a proper girl …' Like them, I'm guessing. '… otherwise I'll never get a boyfriend.'

'Do they have boyfriends?' It's the wrong question – because it shouldn't matter anyway. She's a gorgeous, football-playing, funny, clever tweeny-teeny human, and she can be whoever she wants to be.

'Yeah!' Liv rolls her eyes, as if anybody who's anybody would know that. Fair enough. I realised long ago that I'm not anybody.

I go back to the proper question – the one that I tried to plant in Mr. Warburton's brain on the do-over. 'Isn't there anyone else you can hang out with?'

'No-oooo,' bellows my sister. 'They're my best friends!'

'But best friends don't make you feel bad about yourself, Liv.'

'How do you know?' She's a million decibels by now. Even George is pink with embarrassment. 'You don't have any friends!'

'Olivia!' raps my mum, in her "that's enough" voice.

'What? It's true,' she retorts, although she's a bit quieter about it.

I, meanwhile, am very, very quiet. It is true. It's not even as if the cast members of West Side Story are really my friends, because that was just a dream.

'It's not true.' George reaches over Mum's head to pat me on the shoulder. 'There's Felix, and Charlotte and Cass, and me.' I smile gratefully, but it's not a huge list and they're mostly people I've only just met or they're adults with their own actual lives. 'And those girls at the gate,' she finishes, gesturing up the street towards home.

Girls at the gate?

I see who she means, and my lungs twists so hard I gasp as if I'm trying to make my books bigger. I'm nearly doing Olivia's 'Moves Like Jagger' strut.

India and Suzette are dawdling behind Chief Swisher near our garden fence, angling their heads around Chloe so they can watch us approaching. Chloe, of course, is leading the attack, grinning like a maniac as she leans across the gate slightly. She's inspecting the ramp to the door, and when she sees me and my entourage approaching, her grin widens like a tiger about to pounce and bite off a head. My head.

Instead of biting, she purrs. 'Sashaaaaaaaa!' she coos, like I'm her oldest, dearest friend.

'Who are they?' yells Olivia. 'They look cool!'

'No, they're ...' I can't say they're not cool in case she repeats it on LOUD, so I fumble for some explanation. 'They're girls from school.'

At that, India emits a little laugh like a cough, or possibly a spit. 'We're not just girls from school, Sasha. I'm India?' She simpers at George, obviously thinking she's the person with authority. 'But you might know me as Maria? From West Side Story? The recent show?'

Liv stares at her glossy lips, mesmerised. 'We didn't go because Sash wasn't in it.'

As Chloe's head pivots from one member of our group to another, India cough-laughs again, because of course Sasha wouldn't be in it, but why would that stop us going?

'And because I'm in a wheelchair,' Mum adds cheerfully. 'That school hall wasn't designed for the likes of me.'

The Swishers actually jump with surprise when she speaks. I've noticed that a lot. Unless you're in the hospital, other people seem to assume that anyone in a wheelchair is mute and/or deaf. Many people have yelled at my mum with slow, deliberate words as if she's not disabled but some kind of life-sized doll, or an unfortunately injured foreign exchange student.

Suzette, at least, has the decency to look a little ashamed for being so startled. She smiles gently at my mother. 'Was it a tummy tuck?' she ask sympathetically. 'My sister said they really hurt!'

Mum glances at me, and I see it dawn on her that I've kept everything about her quiet, on the down-low. Not deliberately quiet, but just to myself.

'Something like that,' she says eventually, as George snorts and moves to steer her through the gate.

Feeling like she's connected on some level, Suzette springs forward and sticks out her right hand. 'I'm Suzette. I'd love to talk to you about it. I'm thinking of getting a—'

149

We don't find out what she's thinking of getting – a brain, maybe? – because she's stuck out the wrong hand for my mum to lift up her own and shake Suzette's. We all gaze at my mum's own right hand lying lifelessly in her lap, until Mum reaches out the other hand and waggles Suzette's fingers. 'I had a wrist tuck as well,' she says kindly. Suzette smiles uncertainly at George's back as the women head into the house and I try, unsuccessfully, to shove Liv up the path behind them.

Chloe folds her arms across her chest, which has clearly seen a lot of Tess-and-Danni-type breathing. 'So what's really wrong with her, Sasha?' For some reason, it sounds like she's accusing me of something.

'She's got M.S. Multiple Sclerosis.'

'Euch!' Suzette wipes her hand down her jeans. 'Is it catching?'

'No—' I begin, but then I remember the genetic marker thing, and that it could be a tiny bit catching for me and for Olivia. 'Not for you,' I finish with a gulp.

What is happening? Why are they here, grouped around my own gate like some evil chaperones at prom? Keeping me from my own house, where I feel safe and can keep everyone else safe too – or at least I could until Cass Ely started stalking me from the garden, and the Swishers cottoned onto it.

Ah. Of course. That's why they're here.

Chloe catches hold of my thought in the exact same moment. Slowly, hair swinging, she begins to nod, then tut, then nod again as if she's just solved a quadratic equation in her head. 'So that's it. That's why Cass is hanging around you.'

'Cass?' repeats Olivia. 'Cass that just drove you up to meet us, Sash?'

'Shhhh,' I start, but India pounces. 'Cass Ely drove you somewhere?'

'In an ambulance, because he works at the hospital sometimes,' blurts Olivia.

'It was … I …'

'Oh, don't worry, India. That makes sense. I get it all now,' mews Chloe again, the big-cat who got the cream. 'He's sorry for her. That's it, isn't it, Sasha? He saw you and your poor, poor mum up at the hospital, and he feels sorry for you. That's why he's hanging around you.' She pats my arm. 'Honestly, I feel a bit sorry for you, too. It's a pity my dad doesn't cover everyday medical stuff or he could fight your mum's case. Shame it wasn't a car accident!'

She smiles at me, so completely convinced of her own rightness and understanding of the whole situation that she's started to feel like she can be generous with me. Mum sick, Cass doesn't really genuinely like me. What possible threat could I be?

But then Liv catches up with what she's saying. 'Our dad was in a car accident,' she bellows grumpily.

'Oh!' Chloe thinks about it. 'Well, maybe I'll talk to my dad then,' she offers magnanimously. 'Is he in a wheelchair too?'

'No, he died,' snaps Olivia.

Suzette pulls on the strap of Chloe's bag. 'Leave it, Chloe.'

'I did hear something about that. So sorry, Sasha and Sasha's sister.' India's lips purse as she casts her mind back. She almost sounds like she means it. 'Didn't he ... wasn't he depressed and ...'

To my astonishment, Chloe's eyes sharpen, almost with pleasure. She can't honestly be happy that my dad died? I can't think that badly of anyone, though - even of Chloe - and then she says, 'Was Cass at the hospital when that happened, too?' Ah. I figure out that she's just lined up another reason why Cass would pity-stalk me. 'He must feel so sorry for you, Sasha. We all do,' she croons with her head on one side.

It is utterly and completely fake. Suzette pulls on her shoulder again. 'Come on, Chloe. Leave them alone.'

Chloe shakes her hand off, annoyed at Suzette for interrupting her show of queenly kindness. It's such a show that she should have been in Westside Story, not India. 'Suze! I'm only telling Sasha that I get it. I mean, we came here to warn her to stay away from Cass Ely, but now we've seen the truth – well, everything's different. You talk to Cass as much as you want, Sasha—'

Her oozy goodness turns into a scream as Liv's foot connects squarely with her shinbone.

'Oh, sorry!' says Liv, not sorry at all. 'I missed the ball.'

'The ball's in your hand!' yells India as Chloe hops around, sobbing.

Olivia claps. 'Hey, you're quick! Is your dad a lawyer, too?'

'You watch it, little girl!' screams Chloe, leaning heavily on Suzette's arm, although I wonder if she'd do that if she could see that Suzette is doing her best not to laugh. 'Watch your back at school. You never know when we might be right behind you!'

Olivia just bounces the football on the pavement. 'Good job I don't go to your school, then,' she says airily. Then she dribbles the ball up the ramp to the front door as if she doesn't have a care in the world.

I, however, have a terrible life and many cares in the world. In fact, I have a few more now than I had even yesterday. Chloe confirms this as she backs away from me with her eyeballs fixed on mine.

'Well, you're at our school, Sasha Baker,' she hisses. 'And you need to stay away from Cass Ely.'

I suck in a deep breath. Wow. It does actually help.

'I don't need your permission to talk to Cass,' I manage to say, although my throat wants to fold itself into a concertina to stop the words getting out. 'He's a friend.'

'We'll see about that,' screeches Chloe – but at least she's leaving, dragged away by Suzette and India, who is still so shocked at Olivia's outrageous put-down that she hasn't managed to speak yet. I walk up the path before my liquid legs or my courage fail me completely and I offer to never even lay eyes on Cass again.

Inside the front door, George is pulling off her nurse's scrubs and Liv is bopping from one foot to the other, still in her football kit. I lean with my head hanging down and hands on both knees like I'm in a sky-diving crisis.

'Are you okay?' says George.

'Fine,' I reply, although I imagine I'm really, really not okay.

'I'm taking Liv to soccer. She might be in time for the second half.'

Liv nudges my dangly arm. 'I might stay after for ice cream with Belle and Sania,' she says. 'Okay?'

'Who are Belle and Sania?'

'They're in the First Eleven. Belle offered to teach me to tackle and Sania's our best striker. They're really awesome,' she adds casually.

I read between the lines. 'And Danni and Tess don't like Belle and Sania?'

Olivia shrugs. 'Who cares?' Well, she did an hour ago. A lot. But now she's seen the future versions of Danni and Tess and decided she doesn't need them. Some current has passed through our sisterliness, and I suddenly feel immensely proud of my blaringly loud sibling. 'George,' she honks suddenly, 'can you bring me home after?'

'I shouldn't, but I will. Seeing as it's you.'

'Thanks, George,' we say together. Over the top of Liv's head, George shoots "Talk to your mother" glances towards the kitchen.

I nod and angle my feet in the right direction, but it takes me a very long time to get to the specially adapted kitchen-diner. I really don't want this conversation. Who are your new friends, Sash? Why don't they know about me? Why aren't you telling me things? Are you worried, Sasha? Are you?

And I swallow back the words I will not say as they rise like acid bile from my belly. Yes, Mum, I'm worried. Actually, worried doesn't begin to cover it. And I don't tell anyone because nobody can help anyway. They can't make you better and they can't bring back Dad, and they can't make my life easier but instead they'll make it much, much harder. And I'm not even seventeen yet, I want to cry. I can't even drive! I can't go and get Liv from football practice or school or anywhere! I can't do anything more than I'm already doing to hold us all together without a hideous crack appearing at the crown of my apparently sweaty head and splitting me apart, straight down the middle. And then what will you do, Mum? And Liv? And all of us? What will you do when I've completely cracked into two?

I give her a weak smile as I enter the kitchen. She's holding out an apple so I can chop it up for her, and I wait for the questions. The sad, sorry questions.

But instead she makes a statement, and it's the last thing I expect to her to say.

'Tomorrow,' she says firmly, 'I'm coming with you.'

'You're ... what?' I think at first she means school, and my head starts shaking all on its own. No. No. Nooooo.

'I loved being out today. And Charlotte was so lovely. So I'm coming with you to The Body Beautiful.'

Is she coming along to protect me? I'm not sure. But I look at her body, crumpled into a wheelchair and letting her down miserably, and really quite a long way from beautiful as most people know it, and she looks so hopeful and pretty and completely decided about it that I tell the tears to flee from eyes once again, then pick up my phone to warn Annette. To let her know. That tomorrow ... well, tomorrow is probably going to be a day like no other.

Chapter 15 Next Body Beautiful Day

Breath away,' sings Mum from the back of George's mini-van. 'Take my breath away! Yeah-eh-ah-eh." I love this song! It's in Top Gun. The first one.'

'Wow, I told you you're old,' I remind her.

'I didn't see it when it first came out!' She sounds a little outraged.

'I did,' grumbles George.

'But it was your dad's favourite classic,' Mum continues.

George yelps in horror. 'Classic? Don't classics have Cary Grant in them, or Katherine Hepburn? Not Tom Cruise and people who aren't yet dead?'

'Sorry, Mum, I made a mistake,' I say into the rear-view mirror, wondering if the dials in this mini-van can predict blood pressure like the ambulance. If so, they might be about to register something interesting. 'You're not old at all.'

'Thank you,' she says primly.

'But George is,' I chirp. Mum shrieks with mock horror. 'Totally ancient,' I add.

George fake-glares at me, trying not to laugh as she manoeuvres expertly through the traffic. 'You mind yourself, lady,' she says. 'I can't throw your mum out of the van, but I wouldn't think twice about doing it to you.'

'Good job we're here, then.'

We've arrived. The Body Beautiful looms large beside us, twinkling like Santa's Grotto among the murky windows of the betting shop, the Mini-Mart and a cheap-and-not-cheerful Turkish diner. George spins the steering wheel to guide us into a disabled spot as I hook the badge over the mirror, in a well-rehearsed routine that we've been through a million times. This time it's in a new location, however, and I feel strangely nervous as I open the salon door as wide as possible to allow the wheelchair in. But Mum's having a good day, so she hobbles in instead, leaning heavily on her cane but proud and upright.

Annette and Charlotte are standing to attention by the counter, as if royalty is visiting rather than the intern's mother and the intern's mother's caregiver.

'Welcome!' cries Annette, beaming her Julia Roberts grin. 'So lovely to meet you, Freya, and you too, George. Sasha and Charlotte have told us all about you, and we're delighted to welcome you to our little salon!'

I'm not sure how much Charlotte has said – possibly a mention of wheelchairs and mammoth eyebrows – but I haven't said that much myself, because … well, I don't. I don't say much about anything to anyone. But it my garbled call with Annette the previous night, I did try to find out if the salon had disabled access (double doors and a ramp at the back of the shop, so not a problem, apparently), and whether she did massages for MS sufferers (not a problem, trained occupational health practitioner before she opened the salon, apparently) and whether she could do a special package for caregivers without much money or time (not a problem, she knew all about that, apparently!).

Mum smiles back at her, and though one eye is a little droopy, she has none of the tremors, shakes and slurry speech that might develop later in the day, or the depression that's made her a bit agoraphobic recently. She's young and pretty and vibrant, like someone I remember from a photo but have not seen for a few years. Maybe I haven't been looking properly.

'Well, you're far too glamorous to stand beside,' she says to Annette.

'Do you want to sit down, Mum?'

'No, Sash. I want to look like Annette,' she tells me. 'And then I'll stand beside her.'

Annette and Charlotte laugh, and it's with totally genuine respect. I love these guys. Love them. 'I do have the advantage of spending all day in a beauty salon, with virtually no customers and a very keen apprentice,' says Annette, pointing to Charlotte. 'Perhaps we could interest you in a facial and make-up session?'

'Yes, please!' yells George, a little too fast.

Everyone laughs again. 'You can wait,' my mum tells her. 'Your hands don't shake the mascara all over your face.'

George frowns. 'What's mascara?'

'It's all right, there are two of us.' Charlotte smiles like a kind, beautiful Grammy winner. 'Shall I take George to Room 2, Auntie Nets?' It's the first time I've heard her call her that in public. It suits them both. I love them. Love them!

'Please do,' replies Annette, 'but only because it gives me the excuse to get to know Freya better.' They're a similar age, and I can see they'll get along. Mum hasn't had a new friend in ages. Everyone's getting new friends … 'Can I call you Freya?'

'You can call me Frankenstein as long as you're applying expensive moisturiser to my poor cracked skin.'

They're all giggling as they disappear into the back rooms, which is when I realise that I don't have anything to do. 'Shall I man the phones?' I call after them.

'Oh, yes, please, Sasha! Woman the phones! Hopefully there'll be millions of calls and two million walk-ins!' calls Annette. 'Help yourself to the nail station in the meantime.'

The door between the salon and the treatment rooms swings shut with a therapeutic whisper. I stare at the phone, which doesn't ring, and then realise that Annette takes all the calls on her mobile anyway. It's probably trilling away in her tunic pocket as she massages oil into my mother's face. No need to woman the phones then.

And there aren't any walk-ins, either, naturally. I wonder if I should make myself useful and do some laundry, but don't want to disturb any of the pampering that's going on in the back rooms. That's a shame. I'm good at laundry. I understand laundry. Being the face of The Body Beautiful … that I'm not comfortable with.

The reception area is immaculate, so without anything better to do, I perch myself on Charlotte's tiny stool at the nail station and study the rainbow of plastic fingernails arrayed on the desk before me. There's every colour under the sun and the sea. I plump for a cheery aquamarine and daub some on my nails, then quickly decide that it's a mistake. My fingers look like they belong on a corpse. Ouch, says my brain, and tries to steer me away from the memory of dead-looking fingers on a dead-looking person, but it's too late, and I start to hyperventilate.

As if he's reading my blood pressure remotely, Cass suddenly appears at the door. He waves through the frosted glass, then shoves the door open and strides in, straight up to the nail station. 'They look … nice.'

'It's not very convincing when you hesitate.' I attack the varnish with a wipe. 'Anyway, they make me look dead.'

'Is that not a look you like?' he says with a straight face.

I start to laugh, then realise he isn't kidding. He's so completely serious, in fact, that he's peering directly down his haughty nose to gauge my reaction.

'Of course not.' Why are you here, I don't ask.

'It reminds you of death? Past, future and possibly present?'

'Cass,' I sigh. 'Why are you here? I've been told to stay away from you, but you have to help me by staying away from me. I know you're not interested in me really—'

'I'm very interested in you! Very interested indeed!'

'You … you are? But as a friend. Because you pity me.'

'Yes,' he says, then 'No, not because I pity you. I don't really do pity.'

I shove myself away from the nail table, splattering Death-coloured nail varnish across the tiled floor. 'Then what emotions do you actually do? Because I'm very confused and really quite scared, and I don't have bandwidth for any more confusion and scary stuff. I've had enough! My dad died, Cass. He actually died! And you must have been there at the hospital because you knew.'

He nods. 'I've been there at the hospital the whole time.'

This is genuinely scary. 'Wow! Are you … are you a patient?' I don't ask if he's from the psychiatric ward in case that sets him off and he tries to stab me with a plastic fingernail, but that's what I'm thinking. Of course. He's nuts. A nutter from the hospital, who saw us all there and decided to stalk me, and that's why he could just walk around the premises without a second glass, because they're all used to the handsome psycho rambling around the wards unsupervised …

'No, not a patient.'

'But you're not a doctor? Or a … a student at my school?'

'I'm not not a doctor,' he replies, scratching his nose thoughtfully. 'I know some stuff. Same with being a student. I'm a student of life. And death.'

Oh my life that's flashing before my eyes. 'Death?'

'You know about death, too, Sasha Baker. From your dad dying on your terrible night, and your mother's shortened lifespan.'

'Yes!' I scream. 'Yes, I do! Thanks for reminding me! And now you're going to kill me? You can't! Who will look after Liv? And my mum for the – wow, can't believe you reminded me about this – last few remaining years of her sadly short life? Why would you do that, Cass Ely?'

Cass stands up, taller than I remember, looming over me. I feel tiny and terrified, and it feels like déjà vu. I've felt this way before. Exactly this way.

'I really have messed this up,' Cass is saying through my mind fog. He grabs my hand and I feel something surge from my wrists to my shoulders, something warm and golden like his eyes. 'That's the last thing I was thinking of. Honestly, Sasha, I didn't—'

'Sasha!' cries the next person to crash though the door. Felix takes in my flushed, frantic face and Cass's knowing expression, then shakes his head like a dog to get his thoughts back on track. 'I'm really sorry! I couldn't stop them.'

Felix's mother shoves her way past him. 'I told her that it was against school policy, but she insisted. I tell you, I've had enough of that place. I might just take Mr Warburton up on his offer. Anyway, hopefully we're in time to get you out of the way.'

'Go, Sash. Go out of the back.' Felix is pulling my hands away from Cass Ely's gentle grip, guiding me past the counter.

'Who's coming? Who is it?' I whisper.

I see her through the 'e' in Body Beautiful. Right now it's E for evil. She's hot on the heels – inevitably – of a little two-by-two squadron of Chloe and Dana, followed by Suzette and India. The door jingles happily as Chloe opens it with her hair – or that's what it looks like as she spins into the salon, flanked by Dana and quickly pursued by the other two. To their credit, both India and Suzette are looking a little uncomfortable with the whole thing. They're leaving it to Chloe and to Dana, who doesn't appear to know any better.

'There, I told you!' screeches Chloe, some wild creature attacking its prey.

Felix folds his arms. 'Are you here for a makeover, Chloe? You look spectacularly ugly.'

'Shut up!' Chloe holds out an immaculate sparkly fingernail. 'I told you! Cass Ely is not going to SkyDivers, and Sasha Baker is using … yes, using! … this salon to cover up their secret relationship. Because he's a … an

164

older person from the hospital! And she's … she's …'
She filches around for some heinous insult and came up
with the best she has to offer. 'She's … Sasha Baker.'

'Chloe Shawford, you are completely out of order,'
cries Mrs Webb.

'You're out of order! My dad says that letting them be
in a relationship is … it's … it's … disappointment of
duty.'

Felix's mother gives her a once-over so withering that
I see for the first time where Felix gets his sarcastic
eyebrows from. 'I believe you might mean dereliction of
duty. Which it's not. And anyway, none of that is true at
all. Is it, Felix?'

Felix glances at Cass, and I sense once again the rivalry
between them, the frenemy vibe. 'Well, to be honest,' he
starts. Cass straightens his ginormous spine. 'I don't
really know if Cass has been going to SkyDivers.'

Cass shrugs. He hasn't.

'But the rest of it – no, none of that is true.'

'Trust you to stick up for Sasha, Felix.' Dana huffs like
a horse, practically stamping her foot.

'Slow up there, perky pony,' I whisper.

Spinning around, Dana thrusts her face towards mine.
'What did you say?'

I don't dare repeat it, so I'm almost glad when the E
for Evil person who has been framed in the doorway,
listening to us bicker, steps into the shop.

'It doesn't matter what she said.' Mrs Stewart pushes
her glassed up to her forehead in an attempt to look

intimidating. 'It never matters what Ms Baker says. She's an annoying blip. That's all. She has never and will never amount to anything.'

Four or five people gasp. I'm astonished to find that I'm not one of them, but India is, and possibly Suzette. Felix, his mother and Cass Ely are a given.

'You really shouldn't be allowed to teach, Paula. I'll be filing a complaint,' says Mrs Webb.

'I wouldn't bother. I have the principal's full support.' Stewart holds up a piece of school stationery with writing so small it's impossible to see what's on it. 'Cass Ely, you can report for duty at SkyDivers to prove you are indeed a student. And Sasha Baker, Work Experience is a privilege for older students who can represent the school with maturity, honour and commitment. You've displayed none of those things. You're suspended, pending further discussions.'

I stare at her horrible pasty face, so smug and self-centred. Maturity. Honour. Commitment. Isn't that all I do? All I have? And what do I have to show for it? A suspension and a black mark against my name which means I'll never get to college, or get a job, or do anything other than be trapped in my life, my terrible vie, for ever and a day.

Cass Ely reaches for my hand. 'Sasha Baker, you don't have to take this.'

Tears spill down my cheeks. 'What else can I do? I'm not you, Cass. I can't just smile and get away with things. I'm responsible for people. I'm … I'm stuck. I'm just …'

Just me. Just hopeless. Just desperately, desperately sad.

'And when did it start?' he whispers.

I wipe my cheek with my sleeve. 'What?'

'When did all this responsibility and stuckness start?'

It comes back to me in a rush of pain. That night. The terrible night. That's when it began.

As the thought solidifies in my brain, Cass nods as if he's seen it through a little window in my forehead. 'Yes. And you know what to do.'

'How?' I ask Cass, who's still hunched over in the doorway between Reception and the Treatment Rooms.

'Ambulance at the back. Through the—'

'—double doors behind the laundry and down the ramp.'

Cass smiles. 'Like I said, you know what to do. Make the most of this moment.'

Before anyone can interrupt us to ask why I'm crouched over talking to Cass's knees, I push the interlocking door open with my back, slam it shut and lock it. Then, with not a thought of back-jiggle or having witnesses to sweaty running or anything other than getting to the back of the ambulance – Cass's ambulance – I run for the double doors and burst through them onto the soft shimmering cobblestones of the alleyway. As I'd known it would be, the ambulance is idling, blocking the entrance, so tightly wedged in that I don't know how Cass managed to get out of the driver's door. The passenger door is jammed right against Annette's laundry window, so I can't get in there either.

The back doors are open, though, and the soft hum of the heart-monitoring equipment in the body of the ambulance draws me towards it. The stretcher bed calls to me. Closing the doors firmly behind me, I climb onto its cloud-like softness and close my eyes. Ten. Nine. Eight. Nobody following. Seven. Six. Nobody here but me. Five. Four. Back to that night. Three. I heave a sigh so deep it feels as if it's emanating from my knees. Two. There is no one. I smile and sigh again.

No one.

No one but me.

No …

Chapter 16 That night

Breathe like it's going out of fashion, why don't you,' someone beside me whispers. 'It's not that boring, is it?'

'It's … no. What?' I open my eyes just as Felix, very close on my right, is rolling his.

'You were practically snoring. Even twitched like someone waking up from a deep, deep sleep.'

That's exactly what I'm doing, of course, but I can't tell him that. Can I? I glance at his face to find he's wearing a strange smile instead of his usual snarky side-eye expression. When he sees me looking at him, his gaze drops quickly and he grabs a handful of Minstrels from the family-sized bag in in his lap.

I try to figure out where I am without being too obvious about it. Minstrels. Sitting side by side in the dark. Cinema, obviously. The film is a couple of years old. What am I doing here? I peer sideways past Felix to see if we're here with anyone else, and he spits out a chocolate.

'Sorry. Did you want one?

'Yes, maybe the one you just coughed up?'

'No, a clean one, I mean, out of the bag—' He rattles the plastic wrapper furiously until someone shushes him and his cheeks flush with embarrassment.

'You think I'm twitchy!' I whisper into his ear, but his twitchiness is on overdrive. He leaps out of the seat, scattering chocolates and popcorn everywhere and causing a tidal wave of angry shushing from the people behind him. 'Siddown, idiot!' bellows a voice.

'Give me a break!' hisses Felix to his unseen heckler. 'I'm nervous, okay?'

Nervous? What is he nervous about? Taking hold of his sleeve, I pull him back into the velvety seat. He stares at my hand and actually gulps. 'Are you even enjoying this film?' he squeaks, sounding like Five-Year-Old Felix of yesteryear.

'She might not be, but we're trying to!' yells Angry Man behind us. 'Shut up or get out!'

'Let's get out,' I suggest. I've seen the film a dozen times in the years since this night, in any case. Why don't I remember seeing it with Felix?

Felix nods and we both stumble out of the row, apologising and avoiding the popcorn missiles being directed at Felix's head. Falling through the doors into the lobby, we both lean on our knees as if we've sprinted, and then start laughing. And carry on laughing. It feels incredibly good to laugh. I'm laughing so hard that I stagger backwards and crash into the bin that's overflowing with cartons and cups and scream like Olivia.

'Seriously? Who makes stupid cinema bins so tall and thin that they can only take more than two cups if they're carefully stacked inside each other?'

'I know!' Felix laughs as he scoops me out of the bin wreckage. 'Or any popcorn cartons at all unless they're folded flat. Someone should report them. They fit zero litter and spread the contents all over the floor around them …'

'And then who leaves them right in the spot that you kick them over when you leave the cinema?'

'Prats, right?' Felix takes out his phone. 'Hello? Cinema police? Yeah, I'd like to report a crime. Yes, your stupid pointy bins have just attacked my … my friend.' He nods seriously, the puts his phone away.

'Are they on the way?'

'That's a *waste* of police time, apparently. Sorry.'

'You're *rubbish*,' I tell him.

'Always have *bin.*'

Man, this is fun. I don't remember how long it's been since I've let out a belly laugh like this. Probably not since that terrible night. Or is it this night? I'm very mixed up, but as I wheeze with laughter and fish popcorn out of Felix's collar, I decide to make the most of the moment as Cass suggests.

'Do you fancy a burger?' I ask Felix, knowing that the answer will be yes.

To my amazement, he shakes his head. 'Feel sick. Too many Minstrels, on top of the nerves.'

'Okay, well, I don't think I managed to get any, so I'll have a burger and you can tell me why you're nervous.'

For some reason, this makes him look extremely hopeful. 'Okay,' he whispers.

'Dude,' I tell him, 'you're being weird.'

'Well, what do you expect?'

I look at him again, with his flushed face and chocolate globules on his favourite Cap shirt, and grin. 'True. You are normally weird.'

He looks as if he's about to argue with me on that one but changes his mind. We walk out of the movie theatre and into the Food Court, doing our usual pretending that we're going to have a salad or sushi or something vaguely good for us before heading straight to the burger counter.

'I'll pay,' he offers.

'But you're not having any!'

'My … my treat,' he says, giving me another strange, glassy look.

'Aw. Thanks!' I tell him as I take the cheeseburger and coke. Maybe something has happened that I don't remember yet. Something that makes him feel extra sorry for me. I decide not to ask what it is and opt for a statement instead. 'You're being very nice tonight!'

Felix watches me sit down in my usual seat and then, weirdly again, instead of dropping into position opposite me, where he normally lies around making snarky comments, he folds himself into the booth beside me. 'It's not very flattering that you're so surprised.'

He's being distinctly odd. We chat for a while as I try and find our usual pace and pattern, but it's disconcerting having him jammed up against my side. I'm noticing things about him that I haven't spotted in years, such as the fact that he's wearing a leather bracelet I made in Year 4 or 5. We'd all made one, but his had been removed from his wrist by the class thug, so I'd given him mine instead. His arms are a lot hairier than I remember, too, which is perhaps why I haven't noticed the circlet of leather before.

'I can't believe you still have that,' I say as I scrunch up the burger wrapping.

'What?'

I flick the leather circlet on his wrist and my nail taps against something metallic. The leather bracelet now has a charm on it. I stare at it, trying to remember where I've seen it before – a rectangle, rather like an envelope, with a small Ace of Diamonds shape in the middle.

It's the token. The one that Cass tied to my shoe. But how? That was months, years in the future. And what is Felix doing with it? A horrible feeling of panic and betray and fear ebbs into my stomach, and I look straight up at Felix to demand an answer.

Which is when Felix tries to kiss me.

I leap backwards out of the way, doing fish-like staring and feeling as if I'm having an out-of-body experience. Which, of course, I am – but this is outrageously out-of-body.

'What … what are you doing?'

Well, I can see what he's doing – he's scrumpling his hands against his face and moaning gently, 'No! Oh my god, what an idiot—'

'Felix! Did you just try to kiss me?'

'I'm sorry! I'm so sorry. I shouldn't have … I just thought with this being a date and everything that you might not mind.' He's crimson to the hairline, apart from two rings of stark white around his crinkled eyebrows that makes them resemble pressable buttons, like a drink dispenser. He's still stuttering and pulling at his earlobes. 'Or … or that you might even like it! I'm … I'm an idiot, like the guy in the cinema said!'

'This is … a date?'

Felix stares at me, slack-mouthed with horror. 'Oh my god,' he says again, 'I should have tried harder. I should have asked you what you wanted to do instead of doing what my mum told me to do. I mean, she's a century old and hasn't done dating since medieval days.'

He doesn't realise that my question doesn't mean "Call this a date, dude?' but actually "Is this really a date? A date that I don't remember that my best bud has planned and asked me out on and that I've clearly agreed to?"

Why don't I remember it? And why has he never mentioned it? And why are we not flipping dating then, two years in the future, when I think … I think I would actually like that, if we could fit it into my terrible life somehow?

'I'm so sorry, Sash. I've ruined my one shot at it!' Poor Felix looks so ashamed and horribly sorry that it's hard not to hug him, but I suspect that would make him panic even more. There's a chance he might cry, and I don't want to push him over the edge. 'Can … can we just go back to being friends? I promise I'll never ask you out again.'

I can feel my head shaking. No, we don't need to do that. Try again, Felix, I want to say. Please don't feel bad and yes, ask me out again, and this time let me remember it and not make you feel terrible for having plucked up the courage to risk our friendship by following your heart. And if you do that, then by the time a tall, golden rock-god shows a bizarre level of interest in me in about two years from now, I won't notice because I'll have a boyfriend. The best boyfriend, who's cute with his eyebrows and sweet because he's been my friend forever and knows everything about me. Everything. Even if I don't know everything about him, such as why he has a strange charm on the home-made jewellery I once gave him…

But before the words can come out of my mouth, my phone buzzes in my jeans pocket. Even though this is kind of a special moment, and I should totally put Felix out of his misery, I pull it out automatically in case it's Mum.

Then I drop the phone and the burger bare spins around me in a riot of red leather seats and blaring order numbers.

Because it's not Mum calling me.

It's Dad.

Chapter 17 That night or day

Brie … the strong one in a brick. Cheddar. Yes, lots of that. Maybe some feta?'

I wake up with such a start that I crack my head on a shelf protruding from the wall of the ambulance. Cass mentions four other cheeses, reels off my address, then puts down his phone – correction, my phone. 'Does that hurt?'

'My dad! My dad was on the phone, and I woke up!' I cry. 'Yes, it hurts!'

Cass pauses. 'I meant your head from where you sat up. The bed must have moved while I drove. You're not meant to be under the medicine cabinet.'

Why is he driving me around? 'Oh my life. You *are* a forty-year-old human trafficker. Please,' I beg him, 'don't take me away from my family. They need me.'

'I'm not doing that. I just removed the ambulance from the back of The Body Beautiful before the horrible woman and even more horrible girls found you.'

'Mrs Stewart! The Swishers! How long have I been asleep?'

'Not long. We're outside your house.'

'Why?'

'I thought you might need to be here.'

'Is my mum back?'

Cass shakes his head like a waking lion. 'Nope. Still enjoying her treatment, along with the care-giver lady. Your sister is at school. Felix is at the salon keeping his mother off the horrible woman. It's just us.'

I can't think straight, possibly on account of concussion, or possibly because of Cass holding me hostage in the back of a stolen ambulance. He's even taken my phone. It looks like every slasher movie I shouldn't have seen, and my heart turns slowly over, ready to dive into my stomach.

He cocks his head instantly, as if he's heard a noise. 'What's wrong with your heart?'

How could he possibly know that my heart just sank? I look around for monitors, but of course it's an ambulance so the vehicle is full of them. Must stop torturing myself, I think.

'Yes,' says Cass. 'You must.'

But I said that in my head.

'Can I have my phone back please?' My whisper is so quiet I'm not even sure he's heard it, but then he smiles and hands the phone back to me. 'Why did you take it?'

'I ordered cheese for you.'

'Wh ... why?'

'It says on your hand that you need to buy cheese. I was just helping you out. I've ordered eight kinds as I'm not sure what type you like. It will all arrive …' He checks his arm but there's no watch there. I realise he's looking at the golden hairs along the marvellous marble outline of his forearm; suddenly they ripple as if a breeze wafted through a wheatfield. 'Now.'

He throws open the doors to the back of the ambulance to the sight of a fancy grocery van pulling up to the kerb, from a fancy grocer's we can't afford to use. The driver gets out, catches sight of us in the medical vehicle, and does a double take.

'All okay?' he calls.

I realise how strange a tableau we must present: me sitting up on a gurney, clutching my head and half-sobbing, and Cass bent in half to get his enormous self into the van. Now's my chance, if I want it. I could shout for help. Tell him about Cass the slasher, or Cass the trafficker. But Cass has reached for my wrist and is checking my pulse like a true medical expert, and suddenly that peculiar and rather wonderful golden warmth is flooding up my arm, across my shoulders, down through my torso, and I know that he may be odd, but he's not bad. In fact, he might actually be very, very good.

'Yes, thanks!' I shout feebly. 'Can you leave it at the top of the ramp?'

'Sure,' he says, parking the wooden crate next to the door. Then he approaches the ambulance with a clipboard, and I wonder suddenly if I'm expected to pay.

'I've paid already,' says Cass. He is most definitely reading my mind.

The delivery guy smiles uncertainly. 'Are you able to sign for it?'

'I think so. I'm sixteen.'

'No, I mean because you're sitting in an ambulance.'

'Oh! Oh, no, I'm fine. Just a … a check-up.'

I scribble my name on the delivery list like I've done on a hundred school forms for Olivia, and hand it back to the Fancy Grocer Guy, but not before I've seen the date at the top. It's a date that is etched into my forever. A date that was two, nearly three years ago.

The date of the terrible night.

And I can see by the way Cass is regarding me steadily with his amber gaze, that he knows what date it is too.

'It's not now,' I whisper. 'I mean, I'm not on today doing work experience at The Body Beautiful. Even though you're here with the ambulance and … and everything.'

Cass shakes his head.

'But I woke up out of the do-over!'

Cass pauses, then shakes his head again. 'The cheese will appear at the right time in the now, though. Because I think you need that in the present, not the past.'

'Cass, please tell me! What's going on? Am I dead?'

Cass leans his head towards mine, and I swim in his eyes for a moment. 'The point is, Sasha Baker, that you're very much alive,' he whispers.

I wonder if he's going to kiss me, as that seems to be a thing at the moment, and I find myself hoping he doesn't. This is lucky, as he doesn't even pucker up, but instead jumps down from the ambulance and holds his hand out for me to follow.

'What was happening in your do-over?' he asks, opening the gate for me.

I don't know how he knows about them, but it suddenly becomes very clear that Cass is not an average hospital orderly and occasional student. His ancientness is breathtaking, and I sense some immense, beautiful power in him that I've only experienced before in tiny doses – in George, and Annette, in Mrs Webb and Felix … and in my dad. It's the feeling I've noticed before around Cass – of being cherished.

'Sasha?' he says again. 'Your do-over was this particular day, yes?'

'Yes,' I tell him, 'but later. Later in the evening. I was with Felix and we … we were on a date! He tried to kiss me and then … and then my phone rang, and it was my dad. And I remember what happens after that phone call, so I think the shock woke me out of it! But I'm … I'm not out of it, am I?'

'No. You're in it, but earlier, as you say.' Cass sighs. 'You see, I'm only meant to be an observer, but instead, as Felix has mentioned once or twice, I've dabbled and interfered, and I believe in some ways that might have made your situation worse. Which is the opposite of my intention!' He pats my hand which is lying on the gatepost, trembling. 'I got too curious about you all, but especially you, Sasha Baker. It might even cost me my graduation!'

'So you are a student?'

He inclines his head. Yes.

'But not at our school?'

He points upward. 'Further north,' he says.

'Cass, who are you? How do you know all this?'

I think I might have an idea, but I don't dare say it in case I sound like a crazy person. A crazier-than-usual person.

'There'll be time for that. Right now, I'd like to help you make the most of a moment – just to try to make up for all the disruption I've caused.'

He smiles enigmatically, and for a moment it's so dazzling that I don't notice what's happening at the top of the ramp. Then I see the door opening, the cheese box evaporating into starlight, and a familiar face appearing in the doorway.

'Are you coming in, Sash?' says my dad, raising a hand to wave at the golden boy who's brought me home from school in an ambulance.

Cass smiles, but he's looking at me, not my father.

It's the do-over of all do-overs. I gaze at Cass, who simply points to the door with his gorgeously beaky nose. 'Now,' he says.

I know it's the only other moment of now I may ever get. Before he can evaporate into starlight, too, I stumble up the path and throw myself into Dad's solid, wonderful arms. He catches me, laughing but gentle, then guides me through the doorway and into the lounge.

'Why are you here? How are you here?' I can't stop the tears from bubbling over onto my cheeks.

'Hey, hey, it's all fine!' says Dad, swallowing hard as he tries not to weep himself. 'George has taken Mum to her appointment, and I'll get back on my feet before you know it. I've even got an interview later. Things are looking up, Sha-Sha.' That's his pet name for me, the one Liv used to use when she was a baby.

'Interview?'

I get it. He thinks I'm asking why he's in the house and not at work, and I remember what a huge thing that was for him, but I don't care about that. I don't think we ever cared about that – the fact that he lost his job and didn't tell us, trying to shield us from the worry. We were proud of him. So proud of him for that.

And suddenly I have a chance to make him understand that.

'That's great, Dad,' I say, giving him a quick hug. 'But maybe you should delay getting a job for a while. Mum loves having you at home, and so do we. Liv and me.'

'We can't manage without the money,' he says. 'I couldn't hold my head up—'

'We can manage without the money, Dad. We need you more than the money.' He frowns, not believing me, but I press on anyway. Who knows how long I have until I wake up? 'Mum tells us all the time how courageous you were to keep going out every day when you'd lost your job, but how the best job you do is being her husband.'

He looks up at me, almost fearful in his desperation to believe me. 'Does she really say that?' he asks eventually.

'All the time. And we do too. You're the best dad in the world. Husband and father. Those are the only jobs you need. Right now, that's all you need to do.'

He's genuinely crying now, brushing tears away from his stubbly cheeks with a sort of sweet fierceness. 'You're just saying that to make me feel better … because I've been a bit down.'

And I take hold of his hands, just like Cass takes hold of mine. 'I know. Of course you have. We've all been a bit down. But every day, you make us all feel better, Dad. We love you, and we know you love us, and that's all that matters.'

He can hardly speak, with his face crinkled with crying but also glazed with a happy glow that seems to pulse from his heart. 'I do really love you all.'

'Love you too, Dad. Love you so much!' I tell him, and then we both cry disgusting amounts, hugging and patting each other's backs until finally it all calms down and we start to blow our noses and even laugh.

It's so long since I heard my father's laughter that I nearly sob again, but I also know what a miracle this is, what a chance I've been given. And it's not over yet.

'Do you want to walk up with me to collect Liv?' I ask him. He's been avoiding it, so the other parents don't ask why he's not at work. In the future, I've figured this out, although I didn't know it at the time.

He smiles slowly. 'I really do.'

And so at her primary school gates we collect Little Liv, who screams with delight when she sees him and charges him like a billy goat, and then we stroll home together in the traces of drizzle that begin to dot the pavements. Mum comes home with George, who doesn't seem to notice the ambulance already parked outside and instead squeezes the mini-van onto the driveway with her superb and effortless skill, helps Mum down from the back and then, seeing the smile on my dad's face, backs up and disappears quickly and without comment.

'Cup of tea, love?' says Dad to his wife.

She pulls his hand against her cheek. 'Wonderful. In a bit. Tired now. Let me just sleep here.' She closes her eyes but keeps smiling.

'Whatever you need,' he says. 'In fact, Sash and I have had a bit of a chat, and if you want me to hold off on the job front, I can be home for a few more weeks.'

'Wonderful,' she repeats, with the tiniest wink in my direction.

'I'll just do this one interview today, seeing as it's organised, but then after that I'm all yours.'

'You're not all mine anyway?' she asks with mock concern.

'Always,' he says. 'Always.'

It's so magical that I want to linger in the kitchen, staring at them - but then there's a knock at the door. I open it to find Felix standing there, wearing his favourite Captain America tee-shirt along with a brave but anxious smile on his face.

'Ready?' he asks.

I know what he's asking now. And I'm not ready. I'm not. Not because I wouldn't want to go on a date with him, but because I know this is a critical, vital moment, and that I can really make this second chance be the chance of a lifetime, of several lifetimes …

I draw in a breath before I try to explain but immediately the walls of the lobby buckle and shift. Before I can tell him that this is just the wrong night, the wrong moment for this, I'm back in the booth of the burger bar, recently kissed by a shell-shocked Felix, staring at my phone which has just come alive in my pocket. Alive with a name I didn't think I'd see again. Alive with Dad.

Chapter 18 The terrible night

Breathe, as she was struggling when Liv found her,' shouts my dad's wonderful voice into the scabby cafe carpet where I've dropped my mobile. 'I'm following the ambulance now. Sasha? Can you hear me?'

Felix grabs the phone and hands it to me, not asking why I'm staring at it as if it's about to detonate.

'Sash?' says Dad.

'Yes!' I whisper. 'Yes, I'm here!' And I was there, just seconds ago, with you – putting it right! I thought I was putting it right!

'Look, don't worry about your mum, she'll have the best care possible.'

No, she won't, Dad, I want to say. The best care is you. And she won't have you. I thought I'd avoided this. I thought I'd created some magical time shift in which this doesn't happen.

'Can you go home and make sure Liv's okay? George is on the way but she was with another client. Seriously, mate, I'm following that ambulance, okay?' he yells suddenly.

I picture him screaming at the driver he's just cut off while talking illegally into his phone. 'Don't!' I shout. 'Calm down, Dad! You're right, Mum will be fine!'

'I know, I know, just these other drivers ...' Dad laughs, and the musical beauty of it makes me sob. 'I should get off the phone.'

No, stay on. Keep talking to me. Keep talking to me from the past. I can hardly breathe myself. 'Probably,' I croak.

'I'll call from the hospital.' There's a pause, and I hear the engine revving before he suddenly calls, 'Oh, Sasha?'

'Yes?'

'Sorry about your date. And from one sensitive guy to another, tell Felix I'm sorry, too. Must have taken everything he's got to ask you out. Hope I haven't ruined it.'

Before I have chance to reply, he switches off.

He knew. They all knew – Mum, Dad, Liv and George, and Mrs Webb, and of course Felix himself. Everyone knew about the date that was happening as the Terrible Night unfolded and yet nobody has so much as mentioned it since.

Felix's eyebrows are asking questions as I put the phone back in my pocket with a hand so shaky it makes my arm judder. 'Mum's having a relapse? Dad's following? Liv home alone so you need to get back?' he asks when I don't say anything.

'Yes. Yes to all of the above.'

'Okay,' says my nearly-but-not-quite-boyfriend. 'We'll Uber home.'

'No!' I shout, because somewhere in my numbed yet quaking brain, I know what else is happening. I know what tragedy is unfolding as one sensitive guy finds out he can't help, that there's nothing more he can do …

'We've got to save Dad,' I tell Felix, fumbling to call an Uber that will be prepared to chase an ambulance across a stormy city.

He stares at me, bewildered. 'You mean your mum?'

'I know what I mean!' I screech, unfairly because it isn't his fault, but we're wasting precious moments. 'There's still time!'

Felix holds up his hands. 'Okay! But what about Liv?' Seizing his own phone, he answers the question himself. 'I'll go. I can be at yours in a few minutes.'

'Liv found my mum,' I tell him. 'She might be a mess.'

He rubs my shoulder, and it feels like the most natural thing in the world on this horrible, unbearable night. 'I'm good with mess.'

'You are. You're great with mess. Where is my Uber?' I scream in frustration.

The little digital car is sliding around the corner towards the restaurant. I try not to substitute the image for something else and sprint for the door, not caring what bit of me jiggles or dribbles or anything. This time it really is the ultimate do-over, and I'm not going to screw this up.

I throw myself into the Prius as the driver smiles a welcome. 'Sasha? Going to the hospital?'

'Yes, but don't go on the motorway, you've got to go on bypass and through the back of town, past the leisure centre and along the old walls.'

He peers at his Satnav. 'It says that's much longer—'

'Please!' I scream. 'Please, just do it!'

If I can get there in time, I can stop him. I can flag him down, grab his phone from him. I can stop him taking the call from the ambulance driver, the one that Mum remembers hearing although she's in too much pain and distress to stop them because she knows exactly how he'll react when he hears those words: 'Your wife's in cardiac arrest. My colleague is giving her CPR until we get to the hospital. You'd better hurry, sir.'

I see the big blue H sign for the hospital up ahead. We're not far off now, but the rain is battering against the wind-screen and I can't see the turn-off.

'Please hurry!' I yell. 'And stop at the corner of Turnham Street. No! That'll be too late. No, the other end. Go down Turnham Street to the junction with the main road and let me out at the corner.'

'That's not the hospital, love. That's an industrial park. Are you sure you want dropping off there?'

'Yes! I'm sure!'

I'm surer than I have ever been of anything. Straight ahead, I see the bleary, shimmering outline of the ambulance, lights on and siren blaring, carrying my poor mum to A and E, with an emergency that is awful and life-threatening but from which, this time at least, she'll recover.

The driver turns the Uber with sickening slowness into Turnham Street and trundles along the rain-slicked, pot-holed industrial lane so slowly I want to shove him out of the car and drive myself. 'Here!' I yell, when I can't take it any longer. 'Let me out here!'

He shakes his head uncertainly but does what I ask. I fall out onto the pavement, sobbing gently, looking out for a banged-up classic Cortina that wasn't built for this kind of urban off-roading, waving at any car that passes in the hope that it's my dad, my poor father, hearing only that his wife might die and he must hurry, hurry, put his foot down and take corners too fast and be unable to do anything at all when the boxy car hits the pavement and flips onto its back, then rolls across the street before colliding with a bus, in an emergency that, unlike my mum's, is awful and life-threatening and that he'll never recover from.

A car rounds the nearby junction at a sickening speed. My heart surges. Surely this must be him? But then I see the tiny row of blue lights flashing at the front of the bonnet, and I remember that a police car was on the scene almost immediately after Dad rolled the car. The cops had been concerned about the erratic driving of the car in front as my dad raced to meet my mother at the hospital …

And at the same moment I hear a dull, hideous crunch of metal in the distance. I'm too late. Too late to save him. To save us. What was the point of it all? Why did I have to go through all that once more, just to lose him all over again? I can't get there in time, or even to the hospital. My own heart might as well be in cardiac arrest, it's grinding so much.

'Cass!' I screech. 'Why is this happening?'

With more pain than it should be possible for one body to bear, I slump onto the oily pavement as the Uber driver runs towards me, shouting. 'Sasha! Are you okay? Sasha! Sasha?'

But it's not the Uber driver. It's Cass, his feet barely skimming the pavement as he runs so gracefully towards me that it's like he's floating.

I'm a sobbing wreck on the pavement, and I don't care who sees it. 'Why?' I clutch at the hems of Cass's jeans. 'Why couldn't I save him?'

I don't know how he knows the answers, only that he is somehow behind this and somehow in front of it as well. That he's projected backwards and forwards until time means nothing and only experiences and emotions anchor me to a moment. This is not a moment I want to be anchored to, and I'm furious with him, with myself, with the world when I shake his leg and scream up the entire length of his extraordinary height. 'I couldn't save him!'

Cass gazes down at me in the slanting rain, a burst of light from the street lamp behind him casting a silvery circle around his head. He drops to the floor in one easy movement and sits beside me, cross-legged, on the pavement. Taking one hand, he rubs the back of it gently and instantly I'm warm again, and the patch of ground we're sitting on becomes as dry as a sandy beach, the sky above us molten and dark and swollen with stars.

'You did save him,' he says.

'He still crashed! Just now! He's died all over again! Why didn't I stay home? I could have stayed home that afternoon instead of going on a ridiculous date and found Mum and stopped him going after her, but I didn't get that chance … you stopped me having that chance—'

'No,' says Cass, kindly but very, very firmly. 'It was just his time. Everyone on earth will come and go, and this was his moment.'

I can't bear to believe it. 'So how did I save him then?'

Cass smiles. 'You made him happy. He'd been so sad, full of shame and regret, but you let him know that he was loved and appreciated and honoured, not for what he provided or did for you all, but for being himself. His whole beingness. That,' he says, nodding as if acknowledging the truth of his own words, 'was one very content human. One of the happiest I've known. You did a really excellent job, Sasha Baker. That saved him.'

I listen and feel calmer. Devastated, but at least a little calmer. 'It didn't save us, though, did it? It didn't save the family.'

'The family doesn't need saving,' he says quickly. 'Believe me. I have observed you over a period of weeks, months, years, lifetimes, through the windows of your souls—'

'And our actual windows.'

'Sometimes. And as a family – well, you're really quite exceptional. Together. Loving. Laughing. Making the most of the moments.'

'Lifetimes? You've watched us for lifetimes? Now you really have to tell me who you are. Some kind of ghost? Am I Scrooge?'

As Cass throws back his mane of mixed metals and roars with laughter, he lights up like an emergency flare. From behind his shoulders, a shimmer of feathers rise into the air as he shelters me from the rain. Wings. He has wings. Wings that can stop rain and create make-overs. Every inch of him glows, reverberating with pulsing orbs of light that join into one and surround him like an aura, especially around his head which is crowned with an arc of light. 'Halo,' I whisper.

'Hello,' he says back. Then he laughs again.

'I thought you didn't do jokes?'

'Not good ones. Usually! But that one was begging to come out.'

'So you're an … an angel?' I can hardly believe I haven't noticed it before, but then I've always expected angels to wear gowns and be holy.

Cass grins. 'Archangel. Archangel Cassiel, known for observation, showing up at low points in human lives, and for supporting the unsupported and unnoticed.'

'Is that me?'

'Is it?'

I think about it. 'It has been. Now, I'm not so sure.'

'You, I admit, were an unusual case. So much more noticed and supported than you ever realised. So much so that...' Cass winces, looking a little angelically embarrassed. 'I became super-curious and decided to tag you. We're not meant to do that. It means we've formed an attachment and can't be impartial.'

'The envelope thing!'

'That's my symbol. My tracker.' Cass produces one from his pocket and hands it to me. 'I interfered far more than I should have done, and nearly got demoted. See. I'm always learning too,' he says with a wry grin. 'Told you I'm still at school.'

'So when did you start tracking me? At SkyDivers?' That was when he'd leaned over my shoe.

'Way before that.' He smiles at the horror on my face. 'Don't worry, I won't track you so closely again. You can give me that back when you're done with it.'

'I might ... I might keep it, if you don't mind. It makes me feel—'

'Cherished,' we say together.

'Sure,' he continues, 'but you don't actually need it. The archangels are always around. You just need to ask.'

'Really?'

'That's how I turned up at Work Experience Day. I was asked.'

'But ... but I don't remember doing that.'

Cass winks. 'Didn't say that you're the one who has to do the asking.'

He leans back against the lamp post and wraps his arm around my shoulders – or maybe it's a blanket, or something softer like a duvet. Wings that can stop rain and create do-overs and fill you with warmth and something else. Comfort. And suddenly he's singing.

'We'll find a new way of living
We'll find a way of forgiving
Somewhere
Hold my hand and I'll take you there
Somehow
Someday
Some—'

'Cass,' I say, closing my eyes.

'Sasha Baker?'

I think at some point I should get off this pavement and go home, or get to the hospital so I can hear what's inevitably coming my way - but for now, I'm snuggled up to a little squishy piece of heaven and I've never felt so comfortable and absolutely cherished in my life. 'Shush, please. I'm trying to sleep.'

'Okay, but you know that's not the end?'

'Of the song?'

'No. Of the do-overs.'

How can it not be the end, I think. What else can be left to re-do?

And I empty my head so much to give myself space to think about it that my mind goes completely, completely blank, and suddenly there's only this. The warm comfort of angel wings, and the hypnotic thud-thud, thud-thud of a heartbeat.

Chapter 18 LE Day

Breathe and huff! Huff huff huff! Come on, Freya. Huff!' It's my dad's voice again, I'm sure of it, though it's oddly muffled.

'You bloody huff!' screams my mother … definitely my mother, although she's a lot more vocal than she's been for a while. Or ever. 'This hurts!'

'Sorry, love, but you're doing so well! She's coming! One more huff!'

Another voice interrupts him. 'Might take a few more than that, Mr Baker.'

'Sorry, Freya, several more huffs.'

'Simon! Shut up!' wails my mother, but she seems to be taking some notice of him, as she suddenly screams, 'Huuuuuuuuuuuuuuuuuufff!' followed by 'Ow, ow, oh, oh,' and some startled sobbing.

I hardly dare open my eyes. Mum and Dad together again somewhere. I lift one eyelid and find myself in a small ward in the hospital, with its over-bright lights and medical staff scurrying around the bed bearing my mum. She's clutching my dad's hand even though she seems, at this precise moment, to despise him. I wonder in a wild surge of hope if Dad has made it to A&E this time after the car crash, because of my time shift. Mum's yelling in agony, and he's supporting her …

But then I look down again, and see that they both seem really young, and also that I appear to be peering in through the roof. Mum starts bellowing again and leans forward, Dad patting her back a bit pathetically and whispering, 'Huff! Huff huff!' as if it's a song that's got stuck on a loop.

'That's it, Mrs Baker. One big push and … there she is!'

The doctor lady picks up a tiny, wrinkly, slimy object the doctor from the bed, and suddenly I figure it out. Not a doctor, a midwife. Not MS pain or even cardiac arrest, but childbirth. And not muffled hearing, but the sounds of a conversation when it's coming at you through a birth canal.

'That's me,' I whisper. 'The baby is me.'

They're looking worried, actually – the midwife and the male nurse who's putting me down and rubbing my tiny back, opening my mouth to clear things out of my pipes. I'm not crying. Why am I not crying? That's what babies to when they're born, isn't it? They let out a shout of indignation when the chilly air hits their membrane-thin skin after their cosy existence of snoozing in a hammock in their mum's womb, sucking their doll-sized thumb.

Not me, though. I'm silent, saying nothing – just as I often am.

The room tips abruptly, the glass plate beneath me angling upwards. I'm watching the scene unfold as if it's in a police cell. I'm the gnarly detective on the other side of the one-way mirror, and what I'm detecting is panic. Mum tries to haul herself upright as Dad grips her hand and stares with terror-filled eyes towards the nurse's station, where several heads are bent over me.

'Why am I not crying?'

Without even checking, I know Cass is beside me. No wonder his face looked familiar. He's always been around. Since the first moment in the hospital, and before, in other lifetimes.

I turn to look at him and nearly tip over. Full Archangel Cass is hovering a few inches from the floor, his incredible feathered wings of silver, platinum, bronze and the faintest hint of gold, beating gently above his head. Although he's still in jeans and a shirt, they're now the same mixed-metals colour of his wings, shimmering as if they're made of water.

'You haven't decided yet,' he says.

'What do you mean? I haven't decided to cry?'

He points to Baby Me. 'You're taking a second or two to decide whether you want to jump into this life or not. All baby souls decide. All babies make a choice. You're just weighing things up a bit later than most.'

Weighing things up. Deciding whether to put on the body of my life, my terrible life – a life in which my mum gets horribly ill and I have to be a carer at too young an age, and where my dad dies trying to help us all and I have to deal with that too. Where my sister loses parents like she loses her Monday knickers, so I have to pick up the slack for that along with the trail of flotsam and jetsam her big personality leaves in her wake. I start to cry – not Baby Me, but Now Me ... here in this strange little back-stage area Me.

'I don't know! I don't know if I can do it!'

Cass wags a finger at me. 'You can definitely do it! You've proved all that. It's just whether you want to or not.'

'But I ... sometimes it's so hard.' My wailing is even louder than my mum's huffing. 'It's hard on my own.' Before he even says it, I know what he's going to tell me. 'But I'm not on my own, right?'

'Not really, though you probably have to ask for help. You have me, for a start,' says Cass, 'and other angels.'

I gasp as an idea occurs to me. 'Is that what my dad is now?'

'No, he's a free and beautiful soul, who also looks out for you. And you have people on earth who are not actual angels but look out for you. All the time.'

I think about it. 'George?' Cass nods. 'And ... Mrs Webb and maybe ... Felix?'

'For sure. There'll be others, too, but you've yet to meet them. If you decide to make the journey.'

He smiles gently towards the tiny baby. The room is in panic; monitors are beeping and doctors rush through the door. The pain and hopeful terror on my parents' faces is unbearable.

'And you have your own personal Guardian angels, of course,' whispers Cass Ely.

'It's up to you, Sasha, but honestly, we're here for you when you need us.'

'Both of us, babes!'

I gasp and spin around to the beaming and beautiful faces of Annette and Charlotte. They both giggle a little bashfully and nudge each other, as if they've been caught in the midst of some mischief.

'You two!'

'Us two,' says Annette.

'But Charlotte, you're totally in love with Cass!' I shout, like crushes are the things that matter right now.

Charlotte's golden skin flushes to a burnt orange. 'I'm in love with everybody, that's kind of our thing,' she tells me, trying not to look at Cass. 'But I admit I did get a bit fangirl over Cass! He's the lead singer of the Lampshades in my world.'

'He's not as good a singer,' I tell her.

Cass stares at me down his eagle nose. 'Rude.'

'So what do you think, Lovely?' Annette turns me towards the hospital ward, where my life hangs on by the slenderest of threads. 'Are you in?'

Her therapeutic fingers massage my shoulders. 'Wow. No wonder I fell asleep when you did that. Angel therapy!'

She laughs. 'Actually, this is plain old human therapy. You can go to classes and everything.'

'So I could learn it for my mum?'

'Or,' says Annette airily, 'Liv could learn it for you. Give you a break!'

'Oh no, I—' I can't, I want to say. I have to look after them.

Annette's voice pierces my mind. 'Think about it,' she says. 'Do you need to help them all the time?'

It's a reflex to say yes. It's who I've become. But then I remember Mum's laughter at Fielding's and her fierce determination to carry on as normally as possible, and Liv deciding all by herself to move on from Tess and Danni to people more like her.

'Maybe … no?'

'And do you think, perhaps,' says Cass, in a that suggests he's telling, not asking, 'that taking care of everyone, and all the tiny details of everything, is how you've protected everyone, including perhaps yourself, when life seems so unfair and uncontrollable?'

I stare at the bizarre and worrying nativity scene in the maternity ward below. Unfair and uncontrollable. That's what this moment is to my parents, right now. I feel the truth of what Cass says, and swallow very hard to stop crying. 'Well, when you put it like that,' I say.

'Maybe time to help yourself, Sweetness,' whispers Annette.

Charlotte pops out a pair of stunning silvery wings and wraps them around us both. 'Panel, it's time to vote!' she cries, as if Cass is Simon Cowell. 'We'll love you no matter what, Sasha. No pressure!'

'Well, there is a bit of pressure. I'd say you have about half a second if you want to pull this off. I'm not a miracle worker, after all,' says Cass.

'Yes, you are,' chorus Annette and Charlotte.

'Well, don't let Sasha know that; she'll use me like a genie,' he drawls in what sounds like a very good imitation of Chloe.

I know he's teasing me, so I tease him back. 'Cass, was that another joke? That was actually good! Angel jokes work for you.'

Cass shrugs modestly, then, casting an eye quickly in the direction of Baby Sasha, he takes my hand. All four of us are intertwined, interlinked, and the golden warmth floods through me from head to toe.

'It's Life Experience Day,' says Cass. 'What are you going to choose, Sasha Baker?'

'I don't know! How are we meant to know?' I'm seriously wavering. 'It's like Mrs Stewart said. I'm no good at anything!'

Charlotte's wings ruffle at the mention of the teacher. 'She's very sad, deep down, that lady. You have to feel sorry for her. And anyway, you are totally, really good at stuff.'

'Like what? Cleaning?'

It doesn't feel enough. It isn't enough. And I know that if it isn't enough – if I'm not enough - I might end up giving this life away to other people.

But Cass, to my immense surprise, kneels on the glass floor so that he's looking up at me. Not by much, but enough to make me feel tall, and a tiny bit special.

'You are good at something,' he tells me firmly. 'You're good at love. Actually, you excel at love. And in the end, that's the only thing you need to be good at. You'll see.'

I think about it – no, I feel about it, and I know he's right. I may not remember this when I'm born, but I'm sure I'll be reminded to tell my dad a million times over how he's loved and appreciated, and to let my mum know she's brilliant and wonderful and so, so strong, and to hug my sweet, sassy sister daily, along with anyone else who gets in my way …

'So what are you going to choose?' he repeats.

And I close my eyes and let go of every atom of tension in one swooshy, head-rush moment. 'I choose my own Life Experience. I choose … me.'

'Nice,' says Cass Ely, as if he was sure of it all along. 'Now ... you know what to do …'

Chapter 19 ME day

B reathe in. Breathe out.

Chapter 20 ME Every Day

Breathe in. Breathe out.

Chapter 21 ME day again

B reathe, Mum. That's it. All the way down.'
'I do know how to breathe, my darling daughter,' says my mum, my now Mum, in mock stern-ness.

I'm standing over her, making her do exercises. I do this most mornings, so it could really be any day of any week, but there's a sense of déjà vu in this scenario. Not that surprising, really – there's been a lot of it about recently. I check the clock on the shelf and the calendar on the fridge in one sweeping glance. 7.20am, so still in good time for ... for whatever I have to do today. I can't see the date properly but someone – Mum, maybe? – has scribbled the word 'WE Day' across today's little box.

'What's this We Day?' I ask my mum. 'Like me-time for all of us? Spa day?'

Maybe we're all off to The Body Beautiful, I think, until I remember that it probably doesn't exist any more ... if it ever really did. I'm suddenly confronted with a mental image of Cass in a genie's get-up of harem pants and a tiny waistcoat getting his nails trimmed, and have to smother a laugh.

Mum's laughing, too. 'Well, obviously not, but that's a nice idea. We'll have to plan something like that. Maybe for your birthday - we didn't do anything much for it last month, did we?'

Before I have chance to reply, Olivia's voice bounces down the stairs. 'Sashaaaaaaaa! Where are my Monday knickers?'

Oh. It's that day. That Monday. That WE day, where WE stands for Work Experience. I wait for my guts to clench at the thought of what's to come, but to my astonishment and relief, they remain un-knotted and calm.

'SASHAAAAAAAA!' honks Liv again. 'Monday knickers?'

Mum is preparing to shout something back to Daughter Two, so I wait for her to start just to check it's what I think it is, and then join in so we can announce it together. 'Wear your Tuesday ones, then!'

Above our heads, a bedroom door is thrown back on its hinges as Liv stomps along the landing to argue with us.

'Oop!' whispers Mum, trying not to laugh. 'You're in trouble!'

'Why am I in trouble? You're the knicker-buying parent,' I tell her.

She flicks me with the tea towel. 'Thanks for reminding me. So here's a thought. Next time let's get her *plain* underwear.'

'That,' I say, 'is genius.'

Liv is in full flow by the time she reaches the kitchen. 'I can't wear Tuesday! It's Monday! That's just wrong!'

'You'll be fine,' Mum says. 'Just tell everyone you're so advanced you're already on the next day.'

'Or maybe even better,' I add, 'suggest that they shouldn't be looking at your knickers.'

Liv is loudly considering these very positive options when George arrives. She blusters through the door with her usual cheery presence, and I can't help myself. I rush over and give her a massive, breath-taking hug. Startled, she stands like a statue for a moment and then suddenly gives me a squeeze in return. 'Morning to you, too!'

'I hope you know how much you mean to us, George.' I let her shake herself loose. 'All of us.'

She arches a humungous eyebrow. 'Are you appreciating me? Like in Liv's mindfulness book?'

I could tell her that I have information about her being an angel on earth, but she'd probably think I was falling sick as well as Mum. No need to worry her. 'I guess I am. Is that okay?'

'Bring it!' she says with a grin. Then she gestures towards the door. 'There's someone to see you, by the way.' Her smile gets a little broader, so I'm guessing it's someone good.

I have no idea who to expect, though, and I'm even more surprised when I find Mr Warburton halfway up the wheelchair ramp. He raises a hand, a little embarrassed. 'Sorry! Bad time?' We can hear Liv outside the house, shouting, 'What if I turn Thursday's into THORSday? Viking knickers!'

As Liv's principal doesn't need to hear about her underwear, I pull the door closed behind me and join him on the wheelchair ramp. It's still early enough that smokey mist is coiling from the grass around his shoes, and even while I'm wondering if he's here to tell me that Liv has been expelled for loudness, I get a sense of mystery, of hopefulness about the day.

'Not too early. We've been up a while. So what's Liv been doing?'

'Actually, it's more like what you've been doing, Sasha.'

My heart sinks again, and I wonder if I should get it a floatation device. All this up and down of the heart can't be good for it. He holds out a few sheets of paper, and I guess what I'm in trouble about. 'Sorry, have I made a mistake with the forms? Only sometimes Mum can't sign them, so I have to do it. It's not forged, or anything.'

Mr Warburton shakes his head, his eyes crinkly and warm but clear. 'These aren't consent forms, Sasha. It's your essay. The one you didn't send to the Trustees.'

Not knowing what to say, I take the A4 off him and glance at the words I'd written last year ... and also a couple of days ago.

'It was probably a bit naughty of me, but I saved your file as you were leaving after Liv's interview last year, and for some reason I got a ... a nudge, I suppose you'd call it ... to find it and read it this week.' The principal

210

looks behind me at our home, and I know he's picturing the things I've mentioned in the essay. 'I knew you might not be able to find the time to stop at the school, so I thought I'd catch you here instead. Is that okay?'

'Well, yes, but I ...' Why catch me? What have I done wrong? 'I don't understand.'

'It's a wonderful essay, Sasha,' he says gently. 'The Trustees have agreed unanimously that you should be invited to the sixth form on a full scholarship, if you'd be interested in joining. I know there's not that much of Year 12 left, but we could do some catch-up sessions and get you into the next production and—' He clamps his mouth shut suddenly. 'Am I getting ahead of myself?'

Like Liv, and like I've just done with George, I want to hug him – but I restrain myself and just smile instead ... a very big smile that makes my cheeks tight and my jaw a little sore. 'I'd love that! Thank you. But you'd better ...'

Suddenly I'm seeing myself in a different light – as a capable student, yes, but also as a daughter and a sister. Liv will like having her Big Sis at the top of the year, and Mum will like having both of us in the same place. She might also enjoy talking to Mr Warburton some more, with his kind, crinkly eyes and willingness to put himself out for his students - especially the students who happen to be her own kids.

I wait for a stab of something possessive and defensive to plunge through me on Dad's behalf, and there is a little something there under my ribs ... but it's only a little something. Miniscule, really. I hear Dad's voice in my head: Huff. Huff huff. I breathe in and out, and the feeling completely disappears.

'You'd better check with Mum,' I tell him.

I'd swear he blushes. 'Oh! Of course.' The school principal suddenly looks a bit skittish, hopping uncertainly up and down the wheelchair ramp, and it's suddenly very clear that he would enjoy talking to Mum, too. 'Shall I come back? Arrange another time? Would she—'

'Give us two minutes,' I say, hoping that's long enough to make sure Liv's not dribbling a ball around the kitchen in her dressing gown, 'and it should be fine for you to come in.'

'You're sure?' he asks, and it feels as if he's asking about more than just an early appointment discussion with the principal. It feels like … are you sure you all want to let me in?

'I'm sure,' I say firmly. Dad approves of us all having another beautiful soul in our lives. I just know it.

With this is mind, I warn Mum who's at the door and help her get her cane, then leave her to chat and Liv to walk up to the school with Mr Warburton. As she's free for twenty minutes longer than usual, I ask George for a lift.

'Yes!' she declares. 'The insurance finally came through this morning, so I'm allowed people in the front! Lucky timing, huh?'

'Miraculous,' I say.

Miraculous stuff. It's like the déjà vu. There's a lot of it about. And if I set about it the right time, I can even manage another miracle today … and this time, all by myself.

Chapter 22 Experience Day ...

Breathe, Sasha. Breathe, you idiot!

This is precisely what I tell myself as I march into school for Work Experience Day – not because I'm late, or worried, or aware of the back-jiggle, but because I'm nervous. Excited nervous. Anticipating nervous. Do-I-really-dare nervous.

I think about the last time it was this time and wonder if I'd dare put my hand up for The Body Beautiful again. Even as the thought flutters through my mind, Annette's voice croons in my head: 'You don't need us for that, Sasha. You already are a Body Beautiful.'

Maybe I'll get Mum and George to open the salon instead, if it's still there, and call it 'The Body Rested and the Spirit Lifted' or something. I'd go like a shot.

Owing to George's lift, and Mum and Liv taking care of themselves a bit, it's so super early that the corridors are empty and echoey. Mrs Webb isn't even at the front desk in the office, which is a bit of shame because I was thinking of practicing my Ninja Hugger moves again.

I slow down as I pass the office window, in case she's crouching for a file or possibly, as she has been known to do, dividing lunch items into perspex tubs to hand furtively to kids who've forgotten theirs, or just never get any. There is someone there, but it's not Lorraine Webb.

It's her son.

Felix is perched on the edge of a table, talking to his arm. I'm about to let him know I'm there when suddenly I hear him mention my name. I lean in closer. It's not his arm he's chatting to. It's the leather bracelet I gave him when we were seven – or rather, the tiny charm on the bracelet I gave him when we were seven. 'She said it would protect me, even though I don't know how,' he's muttering. 'Well, now she might need protecting. I don't know what you can do, but …' He drags in a deep breath, clutches Cass's tracker between his fingers and squeezes his eyes shut. 'Please help Sash not get annihilated at Work Experience Day!' he hisses in a rush, as if it's all one word.

Darn. There goes my heart again. I recall Cass's words. It didn't have to be me that did the asking, he'd said. And it wasn't, because it's never occurred to me to ask for help. It was Felix. Felix with his little prayer to a charm on a bracelet.

'Good morning, Sasha. You're early!' Mrs Webb appears at the back door into the office. She glances from me to Felix. He's perched on the table beside the photocopier, looking as if he might climb into it and try to squash himself to death with the lid, or drop into the shredder. After the slenderest of pauses, she says lightly, 'They're moving Work Experience Day into the theatre. Too many people for the hall. If you head off now, you might get the best bleachers.'

'Doubt it,' growls Felix, although I'm betting he's not angry with the swots who might get to the theatre first, but with himself for being caught by the person he's been saying-and-praying sweet things about.

The corridors are filling up now with the usual hub-bub of noise and bodies beautiful and bulging backpacks. 'Go on, I'm busy,' orders Mrs Webb.

Felix has no choice but to join me as I turn resolutely towards the school theatre.

'Sash—' he starts, but I interrupt him before he has to squirm any more.

'You know that little token thing on your bracelet?'

'The one I was talking to?'

'What? I didn't notice,' I tell him as breezily as possible. 'No, I was just trying to remember when I gave it to you. I remember handing you the bracelet when Spencer Corrigan stole yours.'

'Thanks for reminding me.'

'But I don't remember seeing the charm until …' I pause to gather my courage. 'Until the night of our date.'

He stops immediately, hunching slightly like I've punched him in the stomach. 'You … you remember our date?'

I nod.

'I … we all thought you'd wiped it out of your mind. Because of the Terrible Night.'

'We?'

'Mum. Me. Your mum.' He shrugs. 'We agreed never to mention it again in case it brought back something horrible.'

'You're not horrible,' I tell him with a grin.

'I don't mean me. I mean …'

'It's okay, I know what you mean. But it's all … not fine, it'll never be fine. But different, somehow.'

He frowns thoughtfully, and I wonder if eyebrows can be hugged. 'You're different somehow.'

Kids are starting to barge past us into the theatre, and I know we have to move. 'So did I give you the charm that night?'

'No, when you were moving house and we were changing schools and I was moaning about being in the same place as my mum. You said it would protect me, and that one day, when the moment was right, you'd tell me what it means.'

When the moment's right. Ah, Cass. How he loves his moments. 'Have I never told you?'

He shakes his head, watching me warily, just as someone shoves me in the back.

I spin around, expecting a Swisher, but instead it's Bryony, using her arm as a pretend truncheon.

'Hey, move along there, Maaaria,' she commands in her best New Yoick accent. 'The Giggle Sisters are saving us seats!'

'Bryony! I … I did it!'

She drops her arm and shoots a look across at Felix. 'You told him?'

I have to process this so fast that I find myself staring at her. What I mean by 'I did it' is that, judging by what she's said, I actually did West Side Story. I genuinely went through with it, which is amazing in itself. But what she means is that I've clearly told Felix some special thing that I'm saving for a wonderful moment, and that I've have obviously discussed with her – and probably Ellie and Shannon too – like normal teenagers.

I have friends! I have angels, and guardian angels, and angels on earth … and friends!

I want to do a little dance at the door of the theatre, but instead I just wink at Bryony, smile mysteriously at Felix and seek out Ellie and Shannon. They're slumped along one of the wooden boxes at the back, carefully spreading themselves along it so nobody else can sit down. Chloe and Dana approach when they see the space.

'Move,' says Dana rudely.

'No can do, these are saved for Sash, Bryony, and Felix,' Ellie squeaks bravely.

Chloe gives her a withering stare, but is disconcerted when it just makes Ellie and Shannon splutter with laughter. With a violent flick of her hair, she struts off behind Dana to complain to someone. Anyone.

I look around for Suzette and India. They're close behind Queen Swisher, who looks as nasty as ever, but are talking between themselves and finding a seat apart from the other two. India squeezes in beside Todd Minchin, I notice, and somehow I'm pleased. They were kind of save-able, those two, and it looks like they've made some reasonable choices.

Suddenly Mrs Stewart coughs and steps onto her platform at centre-stage.

'Right! Work Experience Day. If you've already fixed yourself up with something, let me know now so we can free up the other positions. Once that's done, we'll start on the list for the rest of you saddos. First come, first served.'

Chloe sticks up her arm. 'I'm working at Shawford's Law in the High Street,' she carols. 'You can cross me off the list!'

'Of course you are,' snarls Stewart. With a sneer still smeared across her face, she turns to Felix who does his best to turn invisible. 'And Felix Webb, your mother tells me you'll be in the school office.'

'Guilty as charged,' mumbles Felix, to a scattering of sniggers from around the theatre. Man, the acoustics in here are good, I think. I might have possibly sounded amazing!

Mrs Stewart's eyes slide from Felix to me, and she pushes her glasses up onto her forehead in shock. 'Baker! You're actually here.'

I nod as everyone turns to look at me. 'Also guilty as charged.'

With rather nasty glee, the teacher starts flicking over the pages on her flipchart. 'Oh, I've got the perfect thing for you. How about—'

'Actually, Mrs Stewart,' I say evenly, 'I've already got something.'

She stares at me, open-mouthed, and I plough on before my courage evaporates.

'You see, my mum has Multiple Sclerosis, and I've been an official care-giver since my dad died two years ago. Before that, I was an unofficial one.'

'You … I didn't know,' she says in a flat tone, although I'm pretty sure she did because Mrs Webb made Official Announcements on my behalf. Now I think about it, that's possibly how India had heard something about my dad. Definitely listens on occasions. Definitely save-able. 'Still, I'm not sure that counts,' continues Mrs Stewart. 'The point of experience is to try something new, so how about—'

She flips through the list again, but suddenly I stand up.

'Well, actually, the point of experience is to live in the moment and then to learn from it. And anyway, I am trying something new. A new school. I'm going to Fieldings, starting …' I check my wrist, and images of Cass's marble forearm and Felix's bracelet sweep across my mind's eye. 'Now,' I finish.

'Now?' she roars.

A cry goes up from my theatre buddies as they moan about me leaving.

'Okay, after this,' I tell her. Well, I don't want to be too mayhemmy and dramatic and storm out of a packed theatre in front of everyone. I haven't become an entirely different person with my experiences and my learning. Just a stronger version of myself.

Besides, there's something I still have to do.

So I sit through the rest of the job allocation, watching out for any signs of potential bullying from Swishers or Stewart or anyone else, as I'm fairly sure I'll say something this time if anyone is put through what I've gone through.

But I can sense Mrs Stewart easing off – maybe because I've stood up to her and she doesn't have her usual victim to pick on – and the rest of the session passes quickly and without event. Soon we're filing out through the swing doors, picking up our backpacks and trailing off to our classes. A boy I've never spoken to before prods me in the shoulder and tells me he has a sister at Fieldings, and I should look out for her. Her name's Sania, and she's on the football team. 'Nice one putting Stewart in her place,' he finishes with a grin.

'Wow, you're a bit of a celeb,' says Felix as we amble towards the office. He waggles his ridiculous, adorable eyebrows. 'Will you sign my forehead?'

'Sure,' I say, and take out my biggest highlighter.

He ducks out of the way. 'So are you really going to Fieldings right now?'

He looks a little sad, and I suddenly realise that this will all change – the chats in the office, the strolls around the school, the walking home together.

'Not right now. First, I'm going to the Mini-Mart to buy cheese and ham, and then I'll go home and find out what Mum and Mr Warburton have agreed.'

'Sounds like a plan,' he says in a very glum voice.

Now it's just the two of us in the empty, echoing corridor. Two lone figures, spot-lit as they move towards each other. Tony and Maria, but without the tragedy. There's a place for us …

'First, though, I'm going to tell you what the thing on your bracelet means.'

I turn towards him as his eyebrows shoot up to his hairline. 'It's the right moment?'

'The perfect moment.' Somewhere a place for us … I put my hands on his shoulders. 'It means … Felix, you are cherished.'

'Me?' he mumbles, staring straight into my eyes with such a sweet mixture of hope and fear that my own eyes fill with tears.

'You,' I say, and then I kiss him, so he's in no doubt about who's doing the cherishing.

And somewhere above us and around us and inside us, a choir of angels sings.

Hold my hand and I'll take you there

Somehow
Someday
Somewhere.

Then I turn towards a future that is somehow, someday, somewhere magical, and I just … breathe.

The end

Acknowledgements

Normally at this point in a book, the author thanks all the people who know they have helped put it together, at all and any stage in the process. For this particular book, however, I'm going to thank all the people who didn't know they helped me put it together, but without whom BREATHE probably would not exist.

They include a host of teachers, guides and mentors, who for some reason all have names beginning with R. Maybe it's a pre-requisite for spiritual teaching. Thanks, then, to Rhys Thomas, who introduced me to soul purpose; to Robert Ohotto, whose knowledge of archetypes and soul contracts is seemingly limitless; to Radleigh Valentine who speaks wisely of angels; to Robert Holden, who talks my language on soul purpose and on creativity.

Further back, to Dr Robert Maldonado and his wife Debra with whom I embarked on a Jungian hero's journey. Oh, and here's one that doesn't start with R: to John Edward, who underlines constantly the need to tell your loved ones they're loved while they're still here. They all have websites and groups and lessons galore. Go find them.

And to all my beloved family, friends and supporters who uplift my life every day – you are cherished, and I love you.

More YA fiction from Jill Marshall

Pineapple
Fanmail

Teen fiction from Jill Marshall

The SWAGG ensemble series
SWAGG 1: Spook
SWAGG 2: School of ICE
SWAGG 3: Sorcery
SWAGG 4: Soulforce

The Jane Blonde series
Jane Blonde, Sensational Spylet
Jane Blonde Spies Trouble
Jane Blonde, Twice the Spylet
Jane Blonde, Spylet on Ice
Jane Blonde, Goldenspy
Jane Blonde, Spy in the Sky
Jane Blonde, Spylets are Forever

Jack BC in the Doghead trilogy
1 Jack BC, Doghead
2. Jack BC, Dogfight
3. Jack BC, Dogstar

The Legend of Matilda Peppercorn
TLOMP 1, Catgirl
TLOMP 2, Toadstone
TLOMP 3, Questioner
TLOMP 4, Trinity

Stein & Frank: Battle of the Undead People-Eaters

Also by Jill Marshall

Available in print, mobi, epub and audio.

For Young Adults
Pineapple
Fanmail
Lena's Fortune

For Adults
The Most Beautiful Man in the World
The Two Miss Parsons
As It Is on Telly

For younger children
Kave-Tina Rox

For more information,
visit www.jillmarshallbooks.com

Follow Jill Marshall Books
on Facebook and Instagram

Email on info@jillmarshallbooks.com

Jill Marshall Books